WHAT THIS **D1409034**

— Provide instruction ... ... w to play blackjack, craps, roulette and baccarat;

— Show you how to get **$100 in casino coupons** for your food, stay and entertainment;

— Give advice on how to save money by revealing the **worst times to play blackjack** - the times when the dealer will almost certainly take your money;

— Identify the **best and worst bets** and explain how and when to make the best bets;

— Offer special advice for gamblers with small bankrolls who want to take a **controlled shot at winning some big bucks;**

— Deliver practical advice on **how to cut the casino advantage in half** on the roulette table;

— Teach you how to choose an **effective betting method** and provide winning methods for beginners and more experienced players;

— Includes three **heretofore unpublished winning methods:** one for blackjack, one for craps and one for roulette;

— Explain the **important money management concepts** of bankroll, betting unit, stop-loss and stop-win and provide instruction on how to use these concepts to reduce losing sessions and increase winning sessions;

— Show why most gamblers lose because of a loss of self-control and provide a **strategy to maintain your self-control at the tables;**

— Teach you how to **manage your time and play on your terms,** rather than the casinos;

— Document **startling new revelations** on two of gambling's "sacred cows" - when **not** to play blackjack's basic strategy and when **not** to take the odds at the craps table;

— **Expose the myths and mystique of card-counting** and explain why card-counting does not always work;

— Deliver practical advice on choosing Video Poker machines that will **minimize your losses and give you the best odds of winning money;**

— Give all the advice you need for **getting in, getting the money and getting out;**

— Introduce you to *The Casino Gamblers' Network*^{tm}, a group established to help you develop, maintain and enhance your winning edge over the casinos.

THE CASINO GAMBLER'S

WINNING EDGE
at

Blackjack, Craps, Roulette, Baccarat & Video Poker

How To Get In, Get The Money And Get Out

BY JERRY PATTERSON
&
NANCY PATTERSON

**ANNOUNCING A CASINO GAMBLERS'
NETWORK** tm

Gambler's Hotline > > > Gamblers' Clinics
Casino Coupons > > > Gambling Tours
Systems & Methods > > > Gamblers' Newsletter

Dedicated To:

All Gamblers Who Seek The Winning Edge

The Casino Gambler's Winning Edge

Copyright (c) 1989 by Jerry L. Patterson
All Rights Reserved
Publisher: Echelon Gaming Corp.
1133 Thackary Court, Box 777
Voorhees, New Jersey 08043
Address All Inquiries To The Publisher

First Printing: June, 1989

Other Books By Jerry L. Patterson
(Published By The Perigee Division of
G.P. Putnam's Sons: NY, NY)

Blackjack: A Winner's Handbook
Blackjack's Winning Formula
Casino Gambling
Sports Betting: A Winner's Handbook
Break The Dealer

ISBN: 0-9605112-2-9

The material in this book is intended to inform and educate the reader and in no way represents an inducement to gamble either legally or illegally.

ABOUT THE AUTHORS

Jerry Patterson played his first hand of casino blackjack in 1956 at Harold's Club in Reno, Nevada and he has played millions of hands since.

His study of the game began in 1961 when he developed the first computer simulation model of the game of blackjack.

Following a successful 20 year career in the computer services area, the last 10 as Vice President and co-founder of his own firm, Jerry retired in 1978 to become a professional gambler.

Jerry has always enjoyed sharing his expertise and knowledge with others, and, in 1978 established The Blackjack Clinic and School Of Gambling. The Clinic has graduated over 10,000 students while scores of other blackjack schools have come and gone. The Blackjack Clinic has earned an esteemed reputation as the oldest and most successful gambling school in the country.

Jerry has authored five previous books on casino gambling and sports betting published by the New York publishing house: G.P. Putnam's Sons. Jerry is also a syndicated casino gaming columnist, and has written for *The New York Daily News, The San Francisco Chronicle, The Philadelphia Inquirer* and *The Los Angeles Herald-Examiner* among many others.

Mr. Patterson is also a Registered Investment Advisor advising clients on both long-term and short-term investment strategies. In addition to his gambling systems, he has developed methods for beating the stock options and futures options markets.

Nancy Patterson, related to Jerry by marriage, is truly a "gambling counselor" having talked with and counseled thousands of gamblers about the achievement of their goals and about overcoming barriers that may be affecting their gambling wins and losses.

She is the connection for all current students making sure that their questions are answered and that nothing prevents them from using the course data correctly and profitably.

Nancy is also a publisher and public relations coordinator. She published and sold over 25,000 copies of Jerry's first two books before auctioning the publication rights to G.P. Putnam's Sons of New York City.

Nancy has arranged for Jerry to appear on scores of radio and TV Shows and for feature articles about him in newspapers from New York City to Hong Kong.

Jerry and Nancy divide their time between homes in New Jersey and the Reno/Lake Tahoe Nevada area.

TABLE OF CONTENTS

Acknowledgements

Many thanks to Frank Grazian for his invaluable advice regarding the layout, structure, content and title of this book.

Special acknowledgement is due Roger Scholl for doing a super job of editing.

And thanks to Esther Kantz for helping out when help was needed.

CHAPTER 1: HOW TO USE THIS BOOK

This book is written to help you stop losing and start winning at the casinos. There are no "easy money" or "get-rich-quick" schemes in this book. But there is sound, fundamental advice on how to play and how to win.

If you are a beginning player, this book will help you understand the rules of play and the player etiquette at the tables.

If you are an experienced player, this book presents three heretofore unpublished methods for winning at blackjack, craps and roulette.

If you are playing with a small bankroll, you will find many good ideas for improving your chances of building your small bankroll into a larger one.

If you have trouble maintaining your self-control at the tables, please read Chapter 11: How to Develop And Use Self-control To Maintain Your Winning Edge.

If you are a high roller, do not put this book aside thinking it will be too basic to satisfy your needs. Take a look at the conditional progression method in Chapter 4 (Blackjack). It is just one example of a winning method that should improve your game.

If you bought this book in a casino bookstore or gift shop and are wondering where to start, check the **back** of each table game chapter: Chapter 4 on blackjack, Chapter 7 on craps, Chapter 8 on roulette and Chapter 9 on baccarat. There you will find a summary of winning methods and ideas in bullet form.

And if you are a Video Poker player or interested in Video Poker, check out Chapter 10 for some interesting ideas on how to attack this very popular game.

Perhaps the most important underlying principle of any casino gambler to grasp involves the concept of time and the casinos' mathematical advantage. The casinos have a mathematical advantage in all the games.

But this advantage applies over the long-term!

Over the long-term the average gambler will eventually lose about $6 out of each $100 bet at the blackjack table; or $1.50 out each $100 bet on the craps table. How long is the long-term? There is no easy answer to this question. But this I will tell you - the long-term is much longer than the average playing session of the typical casino gambler.

So let's forget about the long-term and focus on the short-term. This is where you the player have the advantage over the house. You have control through management of time and money. You decide which casino to visit. You decide which table to play. You decide how much money to take with you and how much money to bet on each hand, roll or spin. And, perhaps most important, you decide when to leave the table and when to terminate the gambling session.

Very few players understand the importance of these key decisions. How to make them is one of the key benefits you need to attain the casino gambler's winning edge.

Reading this book will start you on the road to becoming a winner. But what about the losers? Let's take a look at gambling from the other side of the table.

The casinos love losers and they need a continuous fresh supply just to stay in business. They have enormous operating expenses meaning they must win every day just to stay in business. These expenses include the salaries of the dealers and other employees, the electric and phone bills and the huge fees they pay their entertainers. The odds at the tables are in their favor. But they need more than this mathematical advantage. They need to separate you from your money as quickly as they can. They need turnover; they need you to lose your money and then the next gambler to come in and lose his. They need big money coming in all the time just to pay their expenses and stay in business. Nonetheless, they keep building more casinos and the existing casinos keep expanding. Why? Because they are making hefty profits. And that is because they are able to find a never ending supply of losers.

If you want to continue to contribute to the casinos' daily income and to their growth, then toss this book in the trash right now because it isn't for you. But if you want to separate yourself from the losing masses, read on. We won't have any impact on the casinos' bottom line because there aren't that many of us. But we will have an impact on our own bottom lines; we will experience the joys of winning! And, believe me, it is much more fun to go home a winner than a loser.

This book will get you started on the road to achieving the winning edge. But there is also something else you can do. Let me explain.

I wrote this book to deliver practical data on how to play and how to win for both occasional and frequent gamblers. But I had another reason. To announce *The Casino Gamblers' Network*[tm] a "gamblers group" dedicated to maintaining and enhancing your winning edge.

This is accomplished through evaluating and disseminating winning systems & methods, scheduling gamblers' clinics, connecting gamblers with like interests with other gamblers, maintaining a gamblers' telephone hotline, publishing a gamblers' newsletter and organizing gambling tours and adventures. I think you will find that this is an exciting idea whose time has come. Full details are in Chapter 12.

CHAPTER 2: A GUIDED TOUR THROUGH THE CASINO

When you gamble in a casino, you should consider your gambling decisions as investment decisions. Your objectives in the casino are the same as in any financial investment : minimize your losses and maximize your gains.

Test your knowledge of casino gambling games as investment decisions by answering the following questions:

- In roulette, as played in the Atlantic City casinos, which bets cut the casino advantage in half?

- In craps, which bet pays off at true odds?

- In which casino game can you actually gain a small advantage?

- Do all slot machines drop the same percentage of the money played?

- What are the worst bets you can make?

- In baccarat does the 5% commission charge on winning banker bets make bets on the player more favorable?

Let's walk through a typical casino and find the answers to these questions. Thus armed, you will have a much better chance of winning the next time you visit one.

All casinos have one thing in common: noise. As you walk into the casino, you are confronted with a sea of slot machines and an incessant sound: a distinctive thud as the arm is pulled, followed by the whir of spinning wheels. This action is repeated in quick random succession so that the sound becomes a rhythmic blur in the background. Drop a coin in one and try it out. The result is immediately apparent in the machine's windows where you watch the wheels come to rest. You can drop nickels, quarters, half-dollars and dollars into the slots, but go easy - they don't call them "one-armed bandits" for nothing. Seventeen percent of all the money played goes to the house. Perhaps we had better move on to a table game. Let's try roulette.

The favorite game in the more elegant European casinos, roulette is one of the least popular games in Atlantic City and Nevada because of the increased casino advantage with American rules. However, there's a major difference between roulette as it's played in Atlantic City and the roulette game offered at most of the Nevada casinos. A rule similar to the European rule called "en prison" has been incorporated into the Atlantic City game. This rule works with all the even-money bets: red-black, odd-even, high (19-36), and low (1-18). If either green zero comes up, you lose half your bet and retain the other half. This feature cuts the casino advantage on even-money bets in half-from 5.26 to 2.63%.

Watch a few spins of the wheel before you place your bet. Notice that there are 36 numbers plus a zero and a double zero. Eighteen numbers are red, eighteen are black, and the zeros are green. Purchase chips from the croupier and place a $2 bet on the big red square at the bottom of the roulette betting layout. The croupier spins the wheel in one direction, the ball in the opposite. If the ball drops into any red number, you win $2, black you lose, green you surrender half your bet and the other half is returned to you. The bottom of the layout contains all the even-money bets. You can bet that a number between 1 and 18 will come up, or an even number, a red number, an odd number, a black number, or a number between 19 and 36. If you stay at the wheel for a while, I suggest you stick with these even-money bets to keep the house's advantage to the minimum 2.13%.

Next let's step into the subdued elegance of the baccarat pit. Notice the deeper pile rugs, the richly upholstered armchairs, and the tuxedo-clad croupiers. The game and environment are quiet and calm in the European tradition. The game is easy enough to play and can be learned in a few minutes by examining any of the casino gaming guides (or refer to Chapter 9 herein). Only two simple decisions are required: how much to bet and whether to bet player or bank.

Baccarat is a game for high rollers. At the Atlantic City casinos, minimum bets range from $5 to $20, and at certain games the minimum bet is set as high as $100. Because of this, baccarat is not a popular game. Most casinos offer only a few tables that seat fourteen players each, but it's a good game to play because of the low house advantage: 1.06% net after a 5% commission charge if you bet with the bank, or 1.23% if you bet with the players.

Now saunter over to the blackjack tables. The first thing you notice is that there are few empty seats. Blackjack is by far the most popular casino game, especially so in the Atlantic City casinos, where you will find very good blackjack rules and where it is sometimes difficult to get a seat at a $3 or $5 table. This popularity is due to the fact that blackjack is the only game in which the player can actually gain an edge over the casino.

Blackjack differs from other casino games in that your chances of winning any given hand depend on the cards remaining to be played, and on the clumping of the cards in the shoe (the container from which 4, 6 or 8 decks of cards are dealt). In roulette, each spin of the wheel is an independent event and does not depend on what happened in the past. If red comes up thirteen times in a row, the chances that red will come up on the next spin are still the same. In blackjack, your chances of winning are dependent, to a large extent, on the tens and aces remaining to be played - if the remaining deck is rich in tens and aces, your chances of winning may increase, depending upon the shuffle, clumping and other factors. By employing a playing and betting strategy to take advantage of these favorable occurrences, you can gain an advantage over the house.

Most players, however, do not take the time to understand the fundamentals of the game; thus they contribute to the casino's ever-increasing profit margins from the blackjack tables. The fundamentals are simple enough to learn. At the Atlantic City casinos, you are dealt two cards face up. Only one of the dealer's two cards is exposed. This is called the up-card. The value of your hand is determined by adding up the face value of all your cards (picture cards count ten and aces count one or eleven). You win if your hand has a higher value than the dealer's, or if he breaks (goes over twenty-one) and you don't. The dealer has an advantage over most players because players must decide whether to draw additional cards, called hitting, before the dealer draws. If a player breaks, he loses, no matter what the dealer does later.

There are four decisions you can make after you are dealt your first two cards: split a pair, double down, hit, or stand. You can also take insurance if the dealer's up-card is an ace. The percentage plays for these five decisions have been worked out through millions of computer-played blackjack hands. Called the *basic strategy*, these plays are presented in detail in the chapter on blackjack.

"Winner! Winner! Front-line winner! Take the don'ts, pay the line, it came easy. Coming out, same good shooter. Craps, eleven, any seven, whirl bets, horn bets, high lows and yos, place your bets." "Let's go - throw a seven, shooter." What is all the shouting about? Amidst this excitement you see a cluster of players crowded around a large oblong table. It's craps, the most exciting of the casino games. You get more action at the craps table in five minutes than you can get at the roulette wheel in an hour. This is a game that high rollers play, but it is also fun for the $3 bettor.

Find a $1, $2 or $3 minimum bet craps table with some elbow room and watch the shooter roll the dice. Notice the pass line on the layout, one of the best bets, because the casino advantage is only about 1.4%. You are betting with the shooter, the player throwing the dice. When the stickman announces "come out roll," place a $3 bet on the pass line. A new series of rolls is starting. If the first roll is a 7 or 11, you immediately win your bet and collect $3. If the first roll is a 2, 3 or 12, you have lost your bet. If another number - 4, 5, 6, 8, 9 or 10 - is rolled, it is called a point and the shooter keeps rolling until he either makes his point, in which case you win, or throws a 7, in which case the casino wins. When the shooter has established his point, you may take a free-odds (or backup) bet. This bet is usually no higher than your pass-line bet and is positioned directly behind it on the layout. Because it is the only bet in the casino that is paid off at true odds (see explanation in Chapter 7), it is never announced and there is no place for the bet marked off on the layout. With no house percentage, the free odds on points 4 and 10 pay off at two to one; points 5 and 9 pay off at three to two; points 6 and 8 pay off at six to five.

Whatever game you select, play the **best bets** as listed below, stay away from the worst bets, and with a little luck, you may come out a winner. If you would like to depend on a little more than pure luck, study the game as it's explained in this book. In the table below , the casino advantage can be best understood by considering 100 bets of $1 each. If the casinos advantage is 5% for example, this means that, out of these 100 typical bets, the casino will win 5 bets or $5.

BEST BETS

Game/Bet	% Casino Advantage
Blackjack/Winning Method	-1.5 (Player advantage)
Blackjack/Basic Strategy	0.4
Craps/Pass Line with Full Odds	0.85

Craps/Pass Line	0.41
Baccarat/Bank	1.06
Baccarat/Player	1.23
Roulette/Even Money (Two Zeros)	2.63
Roulette/All Bets (Single Zero)	2.70

WORST BETS

Roulette/Inside Bets (Double Zero)	5.26
Roulette (5-number Bet)	7.89
Craps/Field	5.26
Craps/Propositions	9.17
Slot Machines[1]	11-17
Big Six Wheel	11-22

---

[1] In some Nevada casinos, the advantage is as little as 2 1/2%. Many casinos advertise their favorable slots on their marquees so look for them.

CHAPTER 3: HOW TO CREATE AND MANAGE A CASINO BANKROLL

You're in Las Vegas or Atlantic City on vacation. You have $300 to last you for five days. What should be your money management strategy? Many occasional gamblers find themselves in these circumstances. And for some the vacation becomes an ordeal when the entire $300 is lost in the first two or three days. The proper strategy would be to divide the $300 by 5 and allocate $60 per gambling day. What do you do if you lose the $60 early in the day? Read this chapter for some good ideas. If you win , put your winnings away and don't take them out until the last day of your trip when you might want to take a bigger shot. If you're conservative, get a money order and mail your winnings home on the day they occur.

Creating Your Bankroll

Most gamblers have no concept of what a Bankroll is. When they go to the casino they grab whatever spare money they can get their hands on and hope for the best. If they go with $100 or $200 and lose the entire amount, which happens most of the time, they "create" another bankroll the next time they decide to visit the casino. They keep no records and have no idea how much they have lost over their last few trips, during the last month or the last year. For a number of reasons this is the wrong way to go.

An important step on your road to becoming a winner is to treat your bankroll with respect. But first things first. The first step is to create your bankroll.

Let's first discuss what a bankroll is not. It is not money you can get with a credit card. It is not money you have coming to you such as an income tax refund. It is not what you intend to save over the next few weeks. It is not money you have in the bank or in a savings account. And, except under certain circumstances which will be discussed below, it is not casino credit.

A bankroll is cold, hard cash you have put together for the purpose of gambling. It is kept separate from your other monies; separate from monies you use for living expenses or monies you have set aside for investment purposes. You should keep your bankroll in a safe place. I suggest, depending on size, you keep it in a safe at home or a safe deposit box at the bank.

Now if you don't like handling cash and carrying cash with you, I suggest the following. Open up a line of credit for a minimum amount, depending on your financial circumstances -- for example $500. And use this as your bankroll. Then, when you go to the casino, write a marker for the $500 and use the money as your working bankroll. When you leave to go home and have won money, be sure to buy the marker back. If you have lost and have less than the $500 left at the end of your trip, the $500 marker will either be treated as a check and sent for collection to your bank or you will be sent a bill for the amount. Treat your credit line with respect and don't be tempted to up the line to an amount that you are not comfortbable with. I would suggest that the amount be no more than 2% of your annual salary. If you are making $25,000, that would equal a line of credit of $500; $50,000 would equal a credit line of $1000; and so on.

Terms You Should Know

Now that we have defined a bankroll, let's define the related terms: betting unit, session bankroll, stop-loss and stop-win.

A betting unit is your minimum bet, the bet you start with when you enter a game. A betting unit can be $1, $2, $5, $10 or $25 or higher. Your betting unit depends on your bankroll size. Your betting unit for each game is different and reflects the casino advantage for that game. To obtain your betting unit for each game, divide your bankroll by the appropriate number defined in the following paragraphs.

For blackjack divide your bankroll by 100 or 200 to get your betting unit. For a bankroll of $500, your betting unit is $500/100 = $5. For a bankroll of $1000 your betting unit is $1000/100 or $10. If you are conservative and want to bet less aggressively, use 200 as your divisor: $1000/200 = $5.

For <u>Craps</u>, use a divisor of 200 to get your betting unit. For a Bankroll of $500, your betting unit is $500/200 = 2.5 or $2 1/2. This means that you should be playing at tables with $2 or $3 minimum bets. These tables are found in most Nevada casinos, but are more difficult to find in the Atlantic City casinos. If you insist on playing craps with a bankroll of $500 in the Atlantic City $5 tables, you must not make the Free Odds bet until you start winning (I will explain this in more detail in the discussion on craps in Chapter 7).

For <u>Roulette</u> you should use a divisor of 500 to 1000 to establish your betting unit, with a minimum betting unit of $1. Many Roulette tables offer a minimum bet of $1 on the "outside" bets of red, black, odd, even, high and low. Using a divisor of 1000, a $1000 bankroll yields a betting unit of $1000/1000 = $1; a $2000 bankroll is $2000/1000 = $2. This is your betting unit for all methods discussed in Chapter 8: How To Play And Win At Roulette. Aggressive players can use the lower divisor of 500 to double their betting units; if you're just starting or don't want to take too much risk, I recommend using the larger divisor of 1000 (which yields the lower betting unit).

In <u>Baccarat</u>, few tables offer a minimum bet of less than $20. I would use a divisor of 200 and seek out the lower minimum tables usually offering a $5 minimum bet. This would require a bankroll of $1000 to play because $1000/200 = $5. To play with a $20 minimum bet would require a bankroll of $4000 (4000/200 = 20). If you insist on playing at the higher minimum tables usually found in the Baccarat pits with a bankroll of less than $4000, do so under special conditions - after a big win of $500 or more at one of the other games. Take a controlled shot, but with no more than $200 of your $500 win, which will give you 10 betting units. (200/20 = $10)

Session, Session Bankroll and Stop Loss

A *session bankroll* is defined as 20%, or one-fifth, of your bankroll. If you are playing with a bankroll of $1000, your session bankroll is 1000/5 = 200 (or 1000 times 0.2 = 200). This amount is also your session *stop-loss*. If you lose the $200, you terminate the session. I recommend limiting your gambling session duration to no more than two hours; anything more and you start to lose control. At the end of a session, or if you drop a session bankroll, take a break for at least an hour. Go out and take a walk on the boardwalk, have a cup of coffee or take in a bar show. This advice is crucial because it keeps you in control. If you lose your session bankroll and immediately go into pocket for money, who's in control? You or the casino?

There is one exception to this 20% session bankroll and stop loss rule and that is craps. Because of the higher level of action available at the craps table, you must be willing to take a little more risk. I recommend establishing a session bankroll for this game of 25% of your bankroll.

Stop-Win

What is a *session stop-win* and a *trip stop-win*. Your session stop-win is equal to your session bankroll. If your session bankroll is $200, this amount is your winning goal during the session. More conservative gamblers can shoot for 50% of session bankroll; it's up to you. The important idea is to set a goal and stick to it. When you win this amount, terminate your session, take a break and enjoy your win. Exception: you are in a hot table and winning - stay until it cools off. How do you know when it cools off? When you have given back **no more than** one-third of your winnings. If you are up $300 for example, leave with at least $200 profits in hand.

Table Stop-Loss

If your session bankroll is $200 for example, what is your individual table stop-loss? And should you have one? Or should you risk the entire $200 at one table? Yes you should definitely have a table stop-loss. And it is one-third of your session bankroll. Get up and leave the table immediately when this stop loss is touched. And find another table. Some tables are simply "cold."

Progression Betting Method

Each of the games reviewed in this book has a

progression betting method associated with it. A progression betting method simply offers a way to progress or increase your bet. The progression can be based on a win, a loss or on other defined criteria. In blackjack, craps and baccarat progression on successive wins is recommended. In roulette, progression on successive losses is recommended. The specific progression sequences are discussed in the chapters on the games.

Energy Level - Playing When You Are Tired

You must never, never play when you are tired. This is when you are most likely to lose your self control. Play when your level of energy is high and when you feel good. Try to stick to the same eating habits as you do at home, eating similar food at similar times. Be very, very careful with your alcohol consumption. Too much alcohol is the easiest way to lose your self-control. If you've had a few cocktails with dinner and feel like you can win the house, do me and yourself a favor and take just one session bankroll with you and give the rest to your spouse or a friend or leave it in a safe deposit box. All casinos have them.

Special Advice To Small Bankroll Players: How To Overbet Your Bankroll

I realize that many gamblers can't raise more than $100, $200 or $500 for their initial bankrolls and, no matter what I advise about waiting until your bankroll is at a sufficient level to justify a betting unit with the above rules, you are going to take your shot.

First, divide your bankroll into 50 betting units. A $100 bankroll = 50 $2 units; a $250 bankroll = 50 $5 units and a $500 bankroll = 50 $10 units.

Second, do not play any game except blackjack. Make sure that you know basic playing strategy cold; this gives the casino only about 0.5% advantage, better than you can do in any other game.

Third, follow my recommended strategy in Chapter 4 dividing your 50 units into 10 table bankrolls of 5 units each. Do not deviate from this 5 unit stop-loss per table under any circumstances, even if it means not doubling or splitting pairs. The strategy in Chapter 4 stipulates that you win five betting units before implementing a conditional progression on the win side. That is your course of action.

Disaster: What To Do If You Lose Your Self-Control And Drop The Entire Bankroll

You've come to town on Friday evening for the weekend with a $1000 bankroll. By Saturday evening you've had five disastrous sessions and dropped it all. What do you do? If you drove in, run for your car and head for home. If you are waiting for a bus or a plane, find a way to pass the time without rolling a credit card or signing a marker. Treat yourself to a gourmet dinner and take in a show. Believe me, this will prove cheaper than risking any more of your hard-earned money at the tables. Do <u>not</u> go to a restaurant inside the casino. Look in the Yellow Pages and pick a restaurant in town; why leave yourself open to temptation.

Take some time to read or re-read Chapter 11 in this book: How To Develop And Use Self-Control To Maintain Your Winning Edge.

On Sunday morning take a bicycle ride on the boardwalk if you're in Atlantic City (8 A.M. to 10 A.M. bikes are allowed). If you are in Las Vegas, drive up to Boulder Dam or better yet take a ride to Valley Of The Fire (about a 45 minute drive, beautiful country and well worth your time). There are plenty of places to stop and look and to hike if you are so inclined. I guarantee you will love the Valley of The Fire. Most visitors to Las Vegas never give it a thought because it interferes with their action. But you have to take time to smell the roses. And practice your self-control. I should know. My first trip to Vegas was in 1956. It took me 31 years to get to the Valley of the Fire - in 1987. Don't wait as long as I did to enjoy this wonder of nature.

If you are in Reno, drive up to "The Lake" (Lake Tahoe). Or drive to Virginia City - the old mining town reaks of history and interesting sights.

If you can survive this kind of gambling disaster and make a positive experience out of it, you will look forward to your next trip with the knowledge that you possess the self-control to become a winner.

Should You Tip The Dealer?

The subject of tipping is an important part of money management. Because every time you tip you either reduce your win or increase your loss. Let me teach you how to let the casinos pay for your tips and maximize the tips you give the dealer.

Make a bet for the dealer but don't put the bet in front of the betting circle on the blackjack table, or as a separate bet on the craps, roulette or baccarat tables. If you do this, the dealer controls the money, not you. Put the dealer's bet on top of your own. Announce this to the dealer: "You're riding along with me on this hand" (or "roll" or "spin"). If you lose the bet, that's the end of it. The dealer has lost too. But he or she knows that you made the bet, because you announced it.

Now if you win, you have one of two choices. Let's say you have bet $1 for the dealer. You can immediately give this to the dealer after the payoff and leave the other $1 (the one you bet) up for the next hand. Or you can bet the dollar you just won for the dealer on the next hand and let the dealer control the money as usual. But leave the $1 you bet for the dealer on top of your bet for the next hand. I prefer the latter because it gives the dealer a chance to win $2 instead of $1. But you are controlling the money, not the dealer.

The casino forces the dealers to take their bets down after each hand. Why? Because on a hot hand they don't want the dealers' profiting along with the gamblers. But when you control the tip money, the dealer rides right along with you. And they really appreciate it. If you don't understand the above discussion, take out some plastic chips and walk through it a few times. It's easy. And it will save you a lot of money. Because a $1 bet can become $10 or more for the dealer on a hot hand. But it's house money, not yours.

Casino Comps: Yes or No?

A discussion of casino comps in a chapter on money management? Certainly! I have seen a cup of coffee cost a gambler hundreds of dollars. Why? Because they waited for it. When the pit boss comps you to dinner, it takes him some time to get the approval. In the meantime you may be playing at a losing table. But you wait for the comp. And lose a couple of hundred more. Is it worth it? Of course not! If you are ready to leave the table on a losing streak, leave! Don't wait for the coffee or the comp. If the comp is in the works, check back with the pit boss later. Leave the table and let him know: "I'll check back with you."

Ratings

In Atlantic City, if you are betting any kind of

money (or "action") at all, the pit announces to you that they are "rating" you. All this means is that they watch your action and record your average bet size, total action and win and loss in the computer. They use this data to determine whether or not they comp you and how much. But this policy encourages gamblers to play for the house and ignore their own money management polices. I have seen numerous gamblers play beyond a stop loss just because they were being rated. This is silly! No it's more than that; it's stupid! It's OK to be rated, but walk when you are ready to walk. Don't worry about your rating.

Comp Cards

The same advice applies to the comp cards that they hand out in many of the Atlantic City casinos. The purpose of the comp cards is to encourage you to get rated, build up a record of time and action, and qualify for comps. This is fine and you should take advantage of the casinos' generosity. But on your terms, not their's. Leave the table on a table stop loss and forget about the rating. It can be detrimental to your Bankroll.

Money Control

When you are in a game you should be aware of how much money you have in front of you. Suppose you buy into a craps game for $100 and run into a hot table. The dice are passing and your winning chips are accumulating in your chip rack. You have $1 chips and $5 chips mixed together and you have no idea how much you have in front of you. Now the dice start cooling off and you begin to give some of it back. If you are not careful, you might give it all back because you don't know how much you have.

Here is how to control your money. When you are winning, the first thing to do is separate your buy-in amount into a rack or a pile. Count your winnings after each hand, roll or spin or, if the action is fast, when the shoe is being shuffled or during a long payoff at the craps table. Use different colored chips for stop-win amounts, (i.e. use a white $1 chip to segregate $100 of winnings from the rest of your winnings that you are playing with). You can also put your stop win in a different rack or spot than winnings you are playing with. When you hit a stop win and decide to stay at the table, the rule is not to give back more than one-third of your winnings. Money control is extremely important in making these critical decisions and is a key to gaining the winning edge. Practice it!

Summary of Winning Tips And Ideas

- Create your bankroll from cash you can afford to lose and store it in a safe place.

- If you prefer not to carry cash, open up a minimum line of credit that equals about 2% or your annual income. Respect your credit line and do not abuse it.

- Define the betting unit for the game you are going to play. A unique divisor is defined for each game. Divide your bankroll by this divisor (explained in this Chapter) to establish your betting unit.

- Define your session bankroll and your stop-loss for any session as 20% of your casino bankroll. Keep your session duration to two hours or less.

- Gamblers with small bankrolls of $500 or less should divide them into 50 betting units.

- If you double your session bankroll, terminate your session, take a break and enjoy your win.

- When you are in a winning streak at one table, give back no more than 1/3 of the money you have won at this table before leaving the table.

- A table departure is triggered by losing 1/3 of your session bankroll or a stop-loss of 3-6 units.

- Never play when you are tired.

- Don't be tempted to use credit cards or cash checks if you drop your entire bankroll. Relax and enjoy the local sights.

- Tip the dealer by controlling his bet with your

bet, rather than by making a separate bet for him.

- Don't wait around at a losing table for a comp. Come back for it.

- Practice sound money control principles as defined in this chapter.

MONEY MANAGEMENT WORKSHEET:

My initial bankroll is: _____

The game I intend to focus on most is: _____

The bankroll divisor for this game is: _____

My betting unit for my game is: _____

My session bankroll is: _____

My session stop-loss is: _____

My table stop-loss is: _____

My session stop-win is: _____

Comments and ideas for creating my bankroll:

CHAPTER 4: HOW TO PLAY AND WIN AT BLACKJACK

The game of blackjack is played with one to eight decks of cards, shuffled by the dealer, cut by a player and placed in a dealing box called a shoe, after the insertion of a cut card about one-third of the cards in from the back of the shoe to indicate the last hand.

Before a new game begins, the dealer spreads the cards to be used across the table, first facedown so the backs can be inspected for telltale markings, and then faceup, enabling both the dealer and the players to ascertain that there are no extra or missing cards. Standard 52-card poker-sized decks are used, and the four suits have no significance; only the numerical value of each card is important: 2's through 9's are counted at their point value, and all 10's and face cards are valued at ten. The ace is unique, and can be counted as one or eleven at the player's option.

Blackjack

After receiving your initial two cards from the dealer, you determine their value by simply adding them together. A 5 and 3 is eight; a king and 6 is sixteen; and an ace and 7 is either eight or eighteen. If your first two cards consist of an ace and a 10 or any picture card, the hand is a perfect one - a "blackjack" - often called a *natural*. Unless the dealer ties you with another blackjack, you have an automatic winner, and instead of the usual even-money payoff, you are immediately paid one and a half times your bet - if you have $10 up, you receive $15. With a tie, called a *push*, no money is exchanged.

Hard And Soft Hands

All hands not containing an ace are known as *hard* hands, and any hand including an ace that can be valued as eleven is called a *soft* hand. For example, an A-5 is a soft sixteen; if hit with a 2, the hand becomes a soft eighteen; if another card is drawn, for instance a 9, the ace is revalued as one (if it were valued as eleven you would "break") and the final hand now becomes a hard seventeen. Any hard hand of twelve through sixteen is known as a stiff, or breaking hand, because it is possible to go over 21 with the addition of one more card.

Objective

Let's now consider the objective of casino blackjack. Many blackjack books define the objective as getting a hand as close as possible to 21. This is not always true. Your objective is to beat the dealer, and learning this lesson is your first step on the road to becoming a winning blackjack player. It is possible to beat the dealer by holding a hand that totals less than 21 - a 12 or 13, for example. Remember there are two ways to win, by holding a higher hand than the dealer, and by not hitting a breaking hand and waiting for the dealer to break. This is a decision that many beginning players seldom make. Thinking they must always get as close as possible to 21, they hit (take extra cards) more often than they should, thus breaking (a hand with a value greater than 21), losing more often and contributing to the casino edge of up to 6% over the nonsystem player.

Casino rules are defined to give the dealer one major advantage and one major disadvantage. His advantage is that he always draws last. If he breaks after you have broken - in reality a tie - he has already collected your chips, and he does not return them. The dealer's disadvantage is that he *must draw* if he has 16 or less; therefore, with hands totaling 12 to 16, it's possible that the next card may break him. You, the player, can capitalize on this handicap by making judicious decisions about drawing or standing.

While many players lose because they hit too often, other novices, unrealistically hoping for the dealer to break, do not hit enough. These hitting and standing decisions cannot be made by hunch; logic must be used. If the dealer's upcard is 2, 3, 4 or 5, you know he must hit, no matter what the value of his hole (face down) card is; therefore, you should *stand* (refuse any additional cards) on a lower hand value, such as 13, and hope for the dealer to break. On the other hand, if the dealer has a high up-card, for instance a 9 or 10, you would hit and try to get as close to 21 as possible because there is a good chance that the dealer's hole card is also high, and with a hand greater than 16, the dealer must stand. After making your hit and stand decisions, if you haven't broken, you wait for the dealer to deal to the other players and then to himself. Then your bet is paid off at even money if you win, collected if you lose, or left alone if you tie.

Options

The characteristic that makes blackjack unique among all casino games is the many player options. After you receive your first two cards, in addition to the option of hitting and standing, under certain conditions you are allowed to split your hand, double your bet, insure your hand, or if you are not satisfied with your cards, sometimes you can surrender them and get half your money back. Almost all decisions are indicated to the dealer by the way you move your hand or where you play additional chips after your original wager is made. Let's look at these decisions and their signals; just remember in Atlantic City and many other places where multidecks are used, you are never permitted to touch your cards or your initial bet.

Standing

The player always has the option of standing at any time. In Atlantic City casinos as well as in many others, you must give a hand signal rather than a verbal signal. To indicate to the dealer that you wish to stand, simply wave your hand, palm down, over your cards. The dealer will then move on to the next player. In many Nevada games the cards are dealt face down and the players pick them up to play the hand. A standing signal in this game is given by tucking your the first two cards dealt (the ones you are holding in your hand) under your chips.

Hitting

If you are not satisfied with the total of your hand, you may draw one or more cards, as long as you don't break, or go over 21. To call for a hit, either point at your cards or make a beckoning motion with your fingers. In the Nevada face down game, scrape your two cards towards you on the felt to call for a hit. When the hit card breaks your hand, the dealer will automatically scoop up your bet and place your cards in the discard tray, as you have lost, even if the dealer subsequently breaks. If you break in the Nevada face down game, just toss your two held cards to the dealer - face up.

Splitting Pairs

When the first two cards you receive are of equal value, you may elect to split them and play each as a separate hand, drawing until you are satisfied or break. You play first the card on your right, and then the card on your left. Two ten-value cards, such as a king and a jack, can also be split, but when aces are split, most casinos permit only one card to be drawn to each. If a ten-value card is drawn to a split ace, or vice versa, the resulting hand is considered a 21, not a blackjack, and is paid off at 1 to 1. This 21 would tie any dealer 21 but would lose to a dealer blackjack. In many casinos, if a pair is split and a third card of the same rank is drawn, the hand may be resplit. However, this is not permitted in Atlantic City. To indicate to the dealer your desire to split, merely slide up another bet of equal value next to your first wager, touching neither your cards nor the original bet. In the Nevada face down game just turn over your pair and put out the extra bet. In some casinos, including those in Atlantic City, you may double down after you split. This procedure is explained next.

Doubling Down

When you think that with just one more card in addition to your first two you will beat the dealer, you are allowed to double your original bet and draw one - and only one - card. While many casinos will permit you to double down on any initial hand except two cards totaling 21, some restrict this option to hands which total 10 or 11. To signal the dealer your intention to double, place another bet, up to the amount of the original wager, alongside your first bet. In the Nevada face down game, turn your two cards over and put out your extra bet. Since you will always have the advantage when you take this option, you should double for the full amount. Again, to minimize the chances for player cheating, you are not permitted to touch either your cards or your original bet. When you split a pair, many casinos will permit you to double after you draw the first card to each of the split hands.

Insurance

Whenever the dealer's up-card is an ace, before proceeding with the hand, he will ask, "Insurance, anyone?" If you believe the dealer's hole card is a 10 for blackjack, you are permitted to place a side bet up to half of your original wager on the Insurance line in front of you. If, indeed, the dealer does have a 10 in the hole, you are immediately paid 2 to 1 on your insurance bet, but lose your original wager unless you too have blackjack and tie the dealer. You are not really insuring anything; you are simply betting that the dealer's unseen card is a 10. The only time I recommend taking insurance is when you have a blackjack and are past the third level of a winning progression (a succession of winning hands). I'll discuss winning progressions later in this chapter.

Surrender

A few casinos offer the option of surrender. If you are not satisfied with your chances of beating the dealer after seeing your first two cards, you may announce, "Surrender"; the dealer will pick up your cards and collect half your bet, returning the other half to you. This is the only decision in blackjack that is indicated verbally. Where the dealer is required to first check his hole card for blackjack, the option is called "late surrender." If you are permitted to turn in your hand before the dealer checks for blackjack, the decision is termed "early surrender." In many casinos, you must announce your surrender decision before the dealer deals to the first hand.

Dealer's Play

After offering cards to all players, the dealer exposes his hole card. If there are players who still have not broken, the dealer then acts on his hand according to fixed rules, with none of the player options. When the dealer's cards total 17 or more, he must stand, and with a hand of 16 or less, the dealer must hit until he reaches 17 or better. If the dealer breaks, all remaining players win. In most casinos, the dealer must count an ace in his hand as 11 if it will raise his hand to 17, 18, 19, 20 or 21. A few casinos make an exception to this rule and require the dealer to hit A-6, or soft 17. It is important to note that the dealer has no choice in the matter. If all the players have hands totaling 18, 19, 20 or 21, the dealer must still stand with a 17 - an obvious loser. Likewise, if the players show hands totaling 12, 13, 14 or 15, the dealer must still hit his 16 and risk breaking an otherwise winning hand. If the dealer does not break, and reaches a hand between 17 and 21, proceeding counterclockwise from third base, he collects from players with lower hands, pays off at even money the players with higher hands, and pushes or ties those with equal hands, indicating this with a tap of the back of his fingers in front of the player's cards. Players are now free to pick up winnings, if any, and make a new bet as the whole process is repeated.

Basic Strategy

Most occasional gamblers are unaware of the tremendous amount of research that has been done to provide blackjack players with winning strategies. This research has been performed with the aid of high-speed computers by some of the best mathematical minds in the country.

The resulting strategy, designed to win more of your good hands and lose fewer of your bad hands, yields the best, or most profitable, decisions applying to all the blackjack options - standing, hitting, splitting, doubling, and surrendering. To understand the strategy, though, you must remember the three variables involved in making blackjack decisions - your two cards and the dealer's up-card. There are 550 possible combinations of these three variables; therefore, there are 550 different blackjack decisions. Fortunately, many of these decisions are similar, and about 30 rules cover all of them. The following strategies covering single and multideck games vary very little, and occasionally using the rules for your basic game in another game will have only a very small effect on your expectations. (A Learning Package including flash cards and a wallet-sized basic strategy card is included with your *Casino Gamblers' Network*tm Membership package - see Chapter 12.)

BASIC STRATEGY FOR THE ATLANTIC CITY GAME
(MULTI-DECK)
THE DEALER'S UP-CARD

YOUR HAND	2	3	4	5	6	7	8	9	10	A
8	H	H	H	H	H	H	H	H	H	H
9	H	D	D	D	D	H	H	H	H	H
10	D	D	D	D	D	D	D	D	H	H
11	D	D	D	D	D	D	D	D	D	H
12	H	H	S	S	S	H	H	H	H	H
13	S	S	S	S	S	H	H	H	H	H
14	S	S	S	S	S	H	H	H	H	H
15	S	S	S	S	S	H	H	H	H	H
16	S	S	S	S	S	H	H	H	H	H
17	S	S	S	S	S	S	S	S	S	S
A,2	H	H	H	D	D	H	H	H	H	H
A,3	H	H	H	D	D	H	H	H	H	H
A,4	H	H	D	D	D	H	H	H	H	H
A,5	H	H	D	D	D	H	H	H	H	H
A,6	H	D	D	D	D	H	H	H	H	H
A,7	S	D	D	D	D	S	S	H	H	H
A,8	S	S	S	S	S	S	S	S	S	S
A,9	S	S	S	S	S	S	S	S	S	S
A,A	P	P	P	P	P	P	P	P	P	P
2,2	P	P	P	P	P	P	H	H	H	H
3,3	P	P	P	P	P	P	H	H	H	H
4,4	H	H	H	P	P	H	H	H	H	H
6,6	P	P	P	P	P	H	H	H	H	H
7,7	P	P	P	P	P	P	H	H	H	H
8,8	P	P	P	P	P	P	P	P	P	P
9,9	P	P	P	P	P	S	P	P	S	S
10,10	S	S	S	S	S	S	S	S	S	S

H = Hit. S = Stand. D = Double Down. P = Split.

48

BASIC STRATEGY FOR THE LAS VEGAS GAME
(MULTI-DECK)

THE DEALER'S UP-CARD

YOUR HAND	2	3	4	5	6	7	8	9	10	A
8	H	H	H	H	H	H	H	H	H	H
9	H	D	D	D	D	H	H	H	H	H
10	D	D	D	D	D	D	D	D	H	H
11	D	D	D	D	D	D	D	D	D	H
12	H	H	S	S	S	H	H	H	H	H
13	S	S	S	S	S	H	H	H	H	H
14	S	S	S	S	S	H	H	H	H	H
15	S	S	S	S	S	H	H	H	H	H
16	S	S	S	S	S	H	H	H	H	H
17	S	S	S	S	S	S	S	S	S	S
A,2	H	H	H	D	D	H	H	H	H	H
A,3	H	H	H	D	D	H	H	H	H	H
A,4	H	H	D	D	D	H	H	H	H	H
A,5	H	H	D	D	D	H	H	H	H	H
A,6	H	D	D	D	D	H	H	H	H	H
A,7	S	D	D	D	D	S	S	H	H	H
A,8	S	S	S	S	S	S	S	S	S	S
A,9	S	S	S	S	S	S	S	S	S	S
A,A	P	P	P	P	P	P	P	P	P	P
2,2	H	H	P	P	P	P	H	H	H	H
3,3	H	H	P	P	P	P	H	H	H	H
4,4	H	H	H	H	H	H	H	H	H	H
6,6	H	P	P	P	P	H	H	H	H	H
7,7	P	P	P	P	P	P	H	H	H	H
8,8	P	P	P	P	P	P	P	P	P	P
9,9	P	P	P	P	P	S	P	P	S	S
10,10	S	S	S	S	S	S	S	S	S	S

H = Hit. S = Stand. D = Double Down. P = Split.

BASIC STRATEGY FOR THE LAS VEGAS GAME
(SINGLE-DECK)
THE DEALER'S UP-CARD

YOUR HAND	2	3	4	5	6	7	8	9	10	A
8	H	H	H	D	D	H	H	H	H	H
9	D	D	D	D	D	H	H	H	H	H
10	D	D	D	D	D	D	D	D	H	H
11	D	D	D	D	D	D	D	D	D	D
12	H	H	S	S	S	H	H	H	H	H
13	S	S	S	S	S	H	H	H	H	H
14	S	S	S	S	S	H	H	H	H	H
15	S	S	S	S	S	H	H	H	H	H
16	S	S	S	S	S	H	H	H	H	H
17	S	S	S	S	S	S	S	S	S	S
A,2	H	H	D	D	D	H	H	H	H	H
A,3	H	H	D	D	D	H	H	H	H	H
A,4	H	H	D	D	D	H	H	H	H	H
A,5	H	H	D	D	D	H	H	H	H	H
A,6	D	D	D	D	D	H	H	H	H	H
A,7	S	D	D	D	D	S	S	H	H	S
A,8	S	S	S	S	D	S	S	S	S	S
A,9	S	S	S	S	S	S	S	S	S	S
A,A	P	P	P	P	P	P	P	P	P	P
2,2	H	P	P	P	P	P	H	H	H	H
3,3	H	H	P	P	P	P	H	H	H	H
4,4	H	H	H	D	D	H	H	H	H	H
6,6	P	P	P	P	P	P	H	H	H	H
7,7	P	P	P	P	P	P	H	H	S	H
8,8	P	P	P	P	P	P	P	P	P	P
9,9	P	P	P	P	P	S	P	P	S	S
10,10	S	S	S	S	S	S	S	S	S	S

H = Hit. S = Stand. D = Double Down. P = Split.

BASIC STRATEGY FOR THE NORTHERN NEVADA GAME
(SINGLE-DECK)
THE DEALER'S UP-CARD

YOUR HAND	2	3	4	5	6	7	8	9	10	A
8	H	H	H	H	H	H	H	H	H	H
9	H	H	H	H	H	H	H	H	H	H
10	D	D	D	D	D	D	D	D	H	H
11	D	D	D	D	D	D	D	D	D	D
12	H	H	S	S	S	H	H	H	H	H
13	S	S	S	S	S	H	H	H	H	H
14	S	S	S	S	S	H	H	H	H	H
15	S	S	S	S	S	H	H	H	H	H
16	S	S	S	S	S	H	H	H	H	H
17	S	S	S	S	S	S	S	S	S	S
A,2	H	H	H	H	H	H	H	H	H	H
A,3	H	H	H	H	H	H	H	H	H	H
A,4	H	H	H	H	H	H	H	H	H	H
A,5	H	H	H	H	H	H	H	H	H	H
A,6	H	H	H	H	H	H	H	H	H	H
A,7	S	S	S	S	S	S	S	H	H	H
A,8	S	S	S	S	S	S	S	S	S	S
A,9	S	S	S	S	S	S	S	S	S	S
A,A	P	P	P	P	P	P	P	P	P	P
2,2	H	P	P	P	P	P	H	H	H	H
3,3	H	H	P	P	P	P	H	H	H	H
4,4	H	H	H	H	H	H	H	H	H	H
6,6	P	P	P	P	P	H	H	H	H	H
7,7	P	P	P	P	P	P	H	H	S	H
8,8	P	P	P	P	P	P	P	P	P	P
9,9	P	P	P	P	P	S	P	P	S	S
10,10	S	S	S	S	S	S	S	S	S	S

H = Hit. S = Stand. D = Double Down. P = Split.

How To Achieve The Winning Edge At Blackjack

Tip 1: Avoid play for two hours after new cards have been introduced into the shoe game. The reason is that it is very difficult, if not impossible, to randomly shuffle 8, 6 or even 4 decks of cards. Cards tend to clump in certain patterns that make it extremely difficult to win during this two hour period. Remember that new decks are usually introduced into play at the beginning of each shift. Watch the first shoe or two of a game with new cards and you will observe dramatic evidence that this advice really works.

If you are playing early in the day or early in the afternoon, you must determine how long your table has been in play. In Atlantic City they open the blackjack tables farthest from the Boardwalk first. So if you are playing at a table near a Boardwalk entrance at 12:30 P.M., fresh cards were probably introduced very recently into this game and your chances of losing are much higher than they would be if these cards had been in play for two hours or more. IF IN DOUBT ASK a pit person. To get accurate information from them, give them a story. Tell them you are unlucky when playing against fresh cards.

Tip 2: The best advice I can give you about winning is NOT to get locked into a blackjack table. How many times have you seen a player win a big amount and then give it all back? Or lose and go into pocket for more? Changing tables is the most important decision you can make in achieving *The Casino Gambler's Winning Edge* and you will learn why in the next chapter. Set a table departure stop-loss and stick to it. I recommend a stop-loss of between three and six betting units, definitely no more than six and preferably three. Your betting unit for blackjack is obtained by dividing your bankroll by either 100 (aggressive) or 200 (conservative). Look in Chapter 3 for more information on betting and betting units.

Tip 3 pertains to the selection of a winning method. First of all be careful if you decide to learn card-counting. Card-counting is a method involving counting high cards and low cards and then using this information to derive the player's mathematical expectation of winning the next hand and betting accordingly. For a number of reasons, some of which are explained in the next two chapters, card-counting, in today's blackjack game and when employed in the casino, does not yield the player advantage derived by the computers.

Secondly, when you choose a betting method, make sure you are betting up (increasing your bet) on successive wins and not successive losses. With the Martingale System, for example, you are betting up on successive losses and risking your entire bankroll to win just one betting unit.

How To Score With A Conditional Progression Betting Method

Here is a conditional progression which means that you progress your bet on a win **AND** a dealer break. I have seen players using this method, who, betting a $10 unit, have won $6000 or more at one table in less than an hour. The progression is 1, 2, 3, 5, 7, 9, 11. You bet the next level in units when you win **AND** the dealer breaks, go back one level on a loss and start over again on two losses in succession. If you win and the dealer does not break, bet the same amount on the next hand. This method should not be employed at all blackjack tables. Do not implement this progression until you have won at least five units at the table as defined under Strategy Recommendation #2 below.

The theory behind why this method works is explained in the Chapter 6: Introduction To The Target Method.

When you use a progression betting method, you must be prepared to modify basic playing strategy. In general you should never double or split when you pass the third level of the progression. The easiest approach is NOT to put any more money on the table at the fourth level or higher. The reason for taking this precaution is obvious; in many instances a double down or pair split loss will wipe out all of the prior wins accumulated during this progression. So what's the point?

An alternative approach would be to double or split only when your prior winnings will cover the potential loss.

Strategy Recommendation #2: Flat Betting To An Objective Win

If you are a conservative person by nature, the best strategy for playing blackjack is to flat bet -- bet the same amount on each hand with a goal of winning five units. When you reach this goal lock up three of the units and play at this table until you lose the other two. If these other two units reach five again, lock up three more and start the cycle over again. Remember to adhere to your stop-loss of between 3 and 6 units.

Summary of Winning Tips And Ideas

- Learn the strategy for playing the hands that pertains to your home casino area.

- Do not play blackjack at any table at which the cards have not been in play for at least two hours.

- Establish your blackjack betting unit by dividing your casino bankroll by either 100 (aggressive) or 200 (conservative).

- Do not hesitate to get up and leave a table if you are not accomplishing your winning goals. Establish and adhere to a stop-loss.

- If you decide to learn how to count cards, respect the realities of today's casino play and understand that your advantage is not what the mathematical studies have claimed.

- Use the conditional progression betting method that involves increasing your bets on successive wins **AND** a dealer break.

- Do not double down or split pairs after passing the third level of your betting progression.

- Do not take insurance unless you have a blackjack and are past the third level of your progression betting method.

- Conservative players should establish the goal of winning five betting units, locking up three and continuing play with the other two all the while adhering to their stop-loss.

CHAPTER 5: CARD COUNTING IN BLACKJACK
- MYTH AND MYSTIQUE

Questions, Questions, Questions

How many times have you sat at a table in a low count situation making minimum bets and winning hand after hand? When you left the table with a smaller profit than most of the other "unskilled players", did you question the value of the count since it did not alert you to a winning situation? How much more could you have made if you raised your bets as the other players at the table did.

How many times have you lost hand after hand in a high count with your maximum bet out?

Bad runs of cards happen even to professional card counters. There is no greater frustration than betting up when the count sky rockets only to be beaten by the dealer hand after hand after hand.

Have you ever been the only losing player at a table with a high count? Everyone else kept getting the high cards and you kept getting the poor hands?

Has there ever been a time when you lost a lot of money playing heads up (just you and the dealer)? When you walked away from the table did it ever occur to you that the reason no one was playing against that dealer was because the dealer was "hot" and had sent the players scurrying away with their losses?

The reason all these situations develop is because in the real world of casino blackjack, there is such a thing as a biased game. And there is nothing you can do to change the bias since the cards are already situated.

COUNTING IS NO LONGER ENOUGH.

It is well known that card counters have a mathematical edge over the casinos. The QUESTION is: Why does the high count sometimes not work at all and why does the low count (when you are supposed to lose) sometimes produce winning hands?

The ANSWER is: Some games have a bias in favor of the dealer and some games have a bias in favor of the player.

I'm going to explain what I mean by biases and how they effect the count. But first, please bear with me for just a few more paragraphs of background.

The Non-Random Shuffle

Most blackjack books with the exception of my book *Break The Dealer* (published in 1986 by Perigee Books and co-authored with Eddie Olsen), state that card counting has been tested in the computers and that you will win about 1.5% of all the money you bet if you count cards correctly and bet correctly according to the count.

If you are playing within the confines of a computer, that is very true because in a computer the cards are never shuffled at all. There are no cards - only a random number generated by a computer program. It's function is to spit out numbers randomly. Random means that each number has exactly the same chance of coming up as any other.

In the casino, there is no such thing as randomly shuffled cards. The dealer shuffles between 3 and 5 times before dealing a new round. The casino's objective is to keep the game going, take your money as quickly as possible and make room for the next player whom they hope will be another loser.

A study which was published in *The Theory of Gambling and Statistical Logic* concluded you would have to shuffle each deck of cards 26 times to get a random shuffle.

In a shoe game, the number of shuffles per deck would actually be even higher mathematically. Six decks times 26 shuffles per deck would be 156 shuffles per six deck shoe before the dealer could deal. At that rate the casinos would go out of business because the bored patrons would leave.

Comparing the blackjack game of random numbers in a computer to the real game of blackjack with shuffling 3 to 5 times is like comparing apples to oranges. Until I realized this, I thought everything was accurate in the card counting research. In his earlier books he recommended the High-Low Point Count. I still feel that particular count is the best one for the non-professional player. It is simple and easier to use than a multi-level count. That's why we teach it.

But our graduates have an ace in the hole. They can *pick out a table where the count works well*. This has to do with the biases in the game caused by the shuffle. When they find a table that has a bias in their favor, the count works better than ever. This is what the Target Technique in the next chapter is all about.

A Brief Lesson On Card Counting

Since there is a long history behind the tradition of card counting and it's recognition as a valid strategy, I feel I should give you some information about how to count. Once you understand the concept you can understand the problem.

Counting does not take a good memory because there is nothing to memorize. All you have to understand is that there are high cards, low cards and neutral cards in a 52 card deck. In fact there are an equal number of high and low cards.

Low cards are 2 through 6; high cards are 10s, picture cards and aces; neutral cards are 7s, 8s, and 9s.

Here are the values of these three categories of cards:

$$2 \text{ through } 6 = +1$$
$$10\text{s, pictures and Aces} = -1$$
$$7, 8, \text{ and } 9 = 0$$

Starting with zero off the top of a deck of cards, all you do is add $+1$ for each low card you see dealt, subtract a 1 for every high card you see dealt and repeat the count so you won't forget it when you see a neutral card or 0.

As the count goes up it means there are a higher number of high cards remaining to be dealt, and if a count is in the minus area, it means that there are more low cards in the shoe to be dealt. Since a shoe rich in high cards favors the player and a shoe rich in low cards favors the dealer (who has to hit until 17), the count will give you a mathematical assessment of your chances of winning the next hand. If your chances are good, you raise your bet. If they are poor, you lower it or bet the table minimum.

The plus count is a consequence of more low cards being played than high cards and since there is an equal number of each in the deck, a plus count means that there are more 10s and aces remaining in the deck to be played than low cards.

However, there is a significant problem in using card-counting in a casino and that is the non-random shuffle. The shuffle can produce many dealer-biased games which you must learn to avoid if you want to profit as you should.

A dealer-biased table, very common in the casino, is one in which the dealer wins more often than he should. The player cannot seem to do much right. Too often the player receives a high card and a low card as his first two cards. When he hits the hand to give the dealer's high up-card some competition, the player often breaks or the dealer ends up beating him by a point or two.

In a dealer-biased game, you lose money even though the count is high. You keep putting out your large bet and the dealer keeps beating you.

Why The Count Does Not Always Work

Consider the case when you are losing on a high count. The reason is this: the count keeps going up because low cards are being dealt. Low cards favor the dealer and you are playing in the midst of a low card clump (a clump of low cards). The low card clump is a dealer bias.

Now consider the case when you are winning on a low count. The count is minus because high cards are being dealt. You are playing in the midst of a high card clump and winning. This is called a player bias.

Things are working out just the opposite of what they are supposed to, aren't they? Granted it doesn't always happen this way; in a shoe with well shuffled cards the high cards will come out when the count goes up. But in a game with like-card-clumping, betting with the count can be devastating because the high cards just don't come out as low card after low card is dealt and the dealer doesn't break.

These clumps are caused by the non-random shuffle. Insufficient shuffling of eight, six, four or even a single deck of cards produces favorable or unfavorable clumps that can last from one shoe to the next.

The table at which you kept winning even though the count was very low would have been a player-biased game. If it was a really good table it may have been what is termed in the TARGET data (discussed in the next chapter) as a "Dealer Breaking Table".

A "Dealer-Breaking Table" is the strongest of the tables you can find and you can make an incredible amount of money at those tables if you know how to recognize one and how to bet accordingly.

Knowing how to pick those tables is enough, even without card counting, to maintain a large edge over the house. If you count, you could use the Target technique to pick your table. At those tables the count will work very well and you will eliminate the problems mentioned at the beginning of this chapter.

As a card counter, your profits should escalate just recognizing the dealer-biased games so that you could stop your large losses.

The Target Method was designed to exploit the non-random shuffle by giving the player a tool to find the tables biased in his favor and the knowledge of how to stay out of the many dealer-biased games in the casinos. Let me introduce you to it in the next chapter.

CHAPTER 6: THE TARGET METHOD - HOW TO WIN CONSISTENTLY AT THE BLACKJACK TABLES

TARGET (Table, Research, Grading and Evaluation Technique) is a blackjack table selection method invented by Eddie Olsen with my cooperation. I have been using and teaching TARGET since 1982. Although it has provoked controversy because it does not have a mathematical basis, we consider TARGET to be the most significant blackjack tool since the invention of card counting.

TARGET identifies blackjack tables where the players have the advantage over the house. TARGET works because it is not practical today to randomly shuffle four or more decks of cards or even single decks of cards. Biases develop that either favor the player or the dealer. TARGET players learn to detect the highly favorable player-biased tables.

I welcomed the development of TARGET because so many of my card-counting students reported losing too many hands on high-count situations. I also noticed this phenomenon at many of their tables and began asking questions about why the count worked well at some tables and not at all at others. Unfortunately, none of the available blackjack research studies could answer these questions.

Blackjack research programs have used computers to study the game ever since card-counting was invented in 1962. Tens of millions of hands have been played under ideal conditions with a perfect random shuffle. Unfortunately, as mentioned many times herein, a random shuffle does not exist in the real world of casino play. A random shuffle is not likely, since even a single deck of cards must be shuffled up to 26 times to assure random distribution of the cards.

TARGET research on the effects of the nonrandom shuffle took place inside the casino. By observing and recording thousands of hands, and by simulating thousands more, Eddie Olsen, later with the help of my blackjack students and by collecting their data, discovered the characteristics of winning and losing tables. With various types of nonrandom shuffles, we were able to isolate and validate the fourteen TARGET factors that are the linchpins of the method.

Our research proved conclusively what we had suspected: that many dealer-based games occur in high-count situations. This happens because of card clumps produced by certain nonrandom shuffles. For example, low card clumps can produce extremely high-count situations. The counter increases his bet in expectation that the missing high cards may appear: a 20 or blackjack or a face card to his doubled 11. But because of extreme clumping, these high cards may never appear (residing behind the cut card) in this shoe. Or the high cards may be clumped, many showing up on the same round with most players being dealt 20's and the dealer pulling a 20 also. These high cards are now out of play and not randomly available to the player when one is needed.

Like-card clumping can be devastating to a player. The reason is that the dealer hits his hand last. The player will stand on a stiff hand expecting the dealer to break. Playing into a low card clump, the dealer makes hand after hand, breaking much less often than the mathematically expected value (derived from a random shuffle study).

On the other hand, clumping can also be favorable to the player. Many dealer- breaking tables occur on neutral to negative counts. The clump may contain a surplus of rich cards which are contributing to the dealer-breaking activity.

You don't have to analyze or track shuffles to employ the TARGET method. An understanding of fourteen simple factors is all that is needed to determine if the game is a player-based games, and whether or not you should get into the game (or leave the game if the table is deteriorating and the card bias is changing).

Although TARGET can be played without counting cards, it works better if card-counting techniques are employed. But you must use a factor called table integrity to decide whether or not to bet up in a high-count situation.

Card counters enjoy TARGET because it releases them from the constraints of traditional card-counting techniques. No more searching for those elusive head-to-head games; no more playing at odd hours when head-to-head games are supposedly available; no more worries about bad cut-card placement; biases detected by TARGET transcend the shuffle, so the effect of cut-card placement is reduced. The TAR-GET table entry techniques will get card-counters and other blackjack players into many more playable games.

TARGET is a short-term money-making technique. It does not work like traditional card-counting techniques where many hours of play may be required before the mathematics prevail and a player wins money. Through our empirical studies, we have determined that it is possible for a TARGET player to win 80 percent of the time. Table selection is an investment decision. You expect to win at each and every table that you select. On those occasions when a table does not offer a return on your investment, we teach you to cut your losses short and make a hasty departure. Something like a stop-loss technique that is used in stock market transactions.

TARGET's short-term advantages make it possible to play with a smaller bankroll than is required for traditional card counting techniques. This is because your chances of winning in any given session are much higher. We have experimented with a $100 casino bankroll and watched it appreciate to $500 on many occasions. The $100 was lost less than one time in five.

TARGET is a tool that is helpful for high rollers and gamblers even if they do not choose to invest the time to find the player-biased tables. All gamblers need information about when and how much to press their bets no matter at which table they are playing. TARGET gives them this information and provides them with a winning advantage without counting.

A Summary Of The Target Method

The TARGET method is based on the exploitation of the nonrandom shuffle. It is comprised of fourteen factors that the player uses to evaluate a table. The factors indicate whether or not the table is player-biased or dealer- biased. A player-biased table is one in which, because of favorable clumping, the players will win 50 percent or more of the hands. A dealer-biased table is one in which, because of unfavorable clumping, the dealer will win 50 percent or more of the hands.

Because TARGET is a propriety method, marketed by Echelon Gaming Corp. I cannot disclose all of the TARGET factors in this book. But I will give you one example that you can use in your own play.

Consider the chip tray. Assume there are two empty columns in the tray with no chips. What does this mean? It could mean that players have come to this table, bought chips, played for a while and then left the table, neither winning much nor losing much. But it could also mean that the missing chips were won by the players. If this latter condition is the case, we may have a player-biased game. Of course, this one clue alone is not enough to give you conclusive evidence that this is a player-biased table. The TARGET player uses this factor, in conjunction with five or more of the other thirteen factors, to decide whether or not this table is an investment opportunity.

There are various styles of play associated with the TARGET method. Some players scout for biased tables. They use the fourteen factors to decide whether or not to sit down and play. Others play at a table with only a few of the factors and, as long as they are not losing, wait for the other factors to develop. Some player-biased tables can be detected one or two shoes before the bias occurs.

Many TARGET players adopt the Partner Play Style. While one partner plays in a player-biased game, the other scouts for another table in the same casino. If they find a dealer-breaking table, both partners play in the same game.

TARGET works very well in blackjack tournaments. You can't choose your table in a tournament, but you can use the TARGET factors for your betting and playing decisions. One TARGET player won a recent tournament in Las Vegas, claiming more than $56,000 in prize money. Many others have placed quite high.

Blackjack Quiz

If you answer yes to any of the questions below, you should consider taking advantage of the money-making opportunities of the TARGET method.

Have you ever sat at a blackjack table where the dealer was breaking a lot and you could do no wrong? You kept beating the dealer hand after hand?

Were you ever $100 or more ahead while playing blackjack but did not leave the table when the cards turned against you? You gave all your profits back and then some?

As a card counter, have you ever lost hand after hand in a very high-count situation with your maximum bet out and seen your trip's profits go down the tubes?

Have you ever won hand after hand with your minimum bet out? How much more would you have made if you could have known the dealer would keep on breaking?

Are you a would-be card counter who practiced at home but could never master counting? Does winning without counting appeal to you?

Have you ever watched a blackjack player making a tremendous amount of money with seemingly little effort? Picture yourself in his shoes taking the money off the table. With TARGET, this is possible.

If you are interested in finding out more about TARGET, please see Chapter 13 for an outline of my TARGET Instructional Program.

CHAPTER 7: HOW TO PLAY AND WIN AT CRAPS

An understanding of the bets and the layout on the heavy wooden twelve-foot by three-and-a-half foot craps table is the first step in learning how to play craps. Examine the two outside sections. Note that they are symmetrical, so a player can stand anywhere and have access to identical areas. The center section is under control of the stickman with his proposition bets. Using a long stick, he controls the dice, feeding them to the player when it is time for the next roll after all the bets have been made.

There are over thirty different bets on a craps layout, but fewer than half a dozen offer the odds that make craps the game with the best value in the casino, exceeded only by blackjack when played by very knowledgeable players. Let's make a study of the different bets with the idea of getting the most for our money. Then we can discuss how to achieve the winning edge.

Come-out Roll

How do we start? Well, each player has designated spots on the table where his bets are to be placed, either by himself or by the dealer. Once you become familiar with the layout, it's a simple matter to locate and keep track of your bets. The stickman now announces, "The dice are coming out," and one of the players becomes the shooter. Players become eligible to shoot as the dice travel around the table in

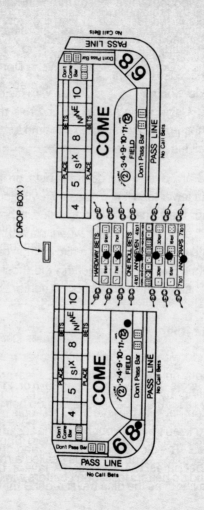

a clockwise direction, and when a new shooter takes the dice, all players make their bets. Because most gamblers bet on the pass line with the shooter, almost everyone at the table pulls for the shooter to "make his point" or throw his winning number before he throws a seven. In craps jargon, this is called "do" or "right"-side betting. "Don't"-side betting, on the Don't Pass Bar 12 line, is also referred to by many craps players as "wrong"-side betting.

Pass Line

To shoot, you must make at least a minimum bet on the pass or don't pass line. Both are shown on the layout. So when the cubes are pushed in front of you, select two and place a wager on the pass line, called the front line by inveterate gamblers, and throw the dice toward the far end of the table. When they come to rest, the numbers appearing skyward are added together and the total is called out by the stickman. The results of the initial throw, called the come-out roll, affect your wagers as well as those of all the other players, since some bets can be won or lost on the first roll.

If the spots on the dice add up to 7 or 11 on the first throw - a natural - the shooter and do bettors win; the don't bettors lose. This is called a pass and the shooter makes a new bet and continues. Should the initial throw total 2, 3 or 12 - craps - called a miss, the shooter and do bettors lose; don't bettors win (except for the bar 12 - 2 sixes on the dice - which is a push) and the shooter does not relinquish the dice, but makes another bet and comes out with a new roll. When the total of the come-out roll is 4, 5, 6, 8, 9 or 10, this number becomes the shooter's point and the number must be repeated before throwing a 7.

After a point is established, a roll of 7 is a loser rather than the winner it was on the starting roll. All numbers, other than the point or 7, thrown in the meanwhile (including 2, 3 or 12 - craps - and 11, a natural) are waiting numbers and do not alter the pass-line wager in any way. Waiting numbers can be used for other betting situations, which will be discussed later.

When the shooter establishes a point, the dealer places a marker called a puck on the appropriate number near the top of the layout. Since there are more ways to make a seven than any other point, the casino now has the advantage and a pass-line bet can't be removed, although a don't-pass bet can. A don't bettor would be foolish to cancel his bet, however, as the odds now favor him. Never make a pass-line bet after the come-out roll, since you have lost the opportunity of winning with a natural 7 or 11 on the opening roll. For a similar reason, the house will not permit a don't-pass bet to be made after the initial roll. You can always tell when the shooter is coming out, as the puck will be resting on the Don't Come line instead of on a number with the dark "off" side faceup.

After the come-out roll, the shooter continues to throw the dice until a decision is reached, regardless of how many rolls he makes. Should the shooter roll his point, he and the do bettors win, and the dealer places an equal amount of chips next to his bet. Always remember to pick up your winnings - if they remain on the table, the dealer may assume you are letting it all ride on the next bet.

After making a point, the shooter makes a new bet and repeats the come-out-roll procedure. After the point is established, if a seven should be rolled, the dealer whisks up the losing bets with great speed and without a "thank-you." The dice now pass to the player on the left of the former shooter and it becomes his turn to shoot.

The pass line is the most popular area on the layout, and it's where some 80 to 90% of all players, mostly due to habit and tradition, make their wagers. The percentage for the house, only 1.41%, makes the pass line one of the best bets in the entire casino. Tips for achieving a winning edge at craps, covered later in this chapter, focus on the pass line as a key bet.

Don't Pass Bar 12

Betting the don't-pass line, often called the back line, is just the opposite of betting the pass line, and is preferred by many veteran gamblers. The bet is made on the section of the layout marked Don't Pass Bar 12, and you are betting against the shooter, which could be yourself. Now the appearance of a natural 7 or 11 on the come-out toss will cause you to lose immediately. But when the cubes dance and come to rest exhibiting a 2 or 3 on top, you will experience the thrill of a win, which pays even money. However, craps 12 is a standoff. Neither the casino nor the don't bettor wins, and the gambler is free to remove his don't-pass if he chooses. It is this remarkable piece of arithmetic which permits the casino to bank all bets whether one wagers with or against the dice.

The house, as you recall, enjoys a positive expectation of 1.41% on the pass line, and through the expediency of barring the 12 on the don't-pass line, the casino realizes an advantage of 1.40%. Thus, the casino holds a slight advantage on both lines.

If you bet the don't pass line, when the shooter rolls a point and then misses out, you win. If he makes his point, you lose. We have learned that most people wager on the pass line. Perhaps only 10% are wrong bettors, possibly because of the pessimistic connotation. It's unnatural for most gamblers not to be able to call with the other bettors for a natural on the come-out roll and for a steady stream of passes. Nevertheless, don't pass is not an erroneous or poor bet; on the contrary, it is one of the best bets in the casino.

If you are a conservative person and have the patience to play the don't side and wait for the outcome without participating in action on almost every roll, I recommend this bet as your best strategy at the craps table.

Come Bets

The come bet, made only after a point is established, is exactly the same as a pass-line bet except you can bet the come any time you want - not just on a come-out roll. Let's say that the shooter has established his point, and he has thrown the dice two or three times and has still not made it. On average, it takes about three and a half rolls to effect a decision and, anxious for action, you bet the come by placing your chips directly in front of you in the come line of the layout. The very next roll of the dice establishes this new bet. If the shooter throws a 4, 5, 6, 8, 9 or 10, the stickman moves your bet to a specific spot in the appropriate number box on the layout, which indicates that it's your bet.

As with a pass-line bet, a come bet cannot be taken down. Of course, if the roll had been 2, 3 or 12, your come bet would have been a loser. An 11 would have won. A come-out roll of 7 would have been a winner, but the pass-line bet would lose. With a come bet in the number box, you are pulling for the shooter to repeat this number before a 7. If he does, you win even money; if he sevens out, you lose. When you win, the stickman places your winnings plus your original bet in front of you on the come line. Be sure to pick it up before the next roll of the dice or you will have a new come bet for the total amount.

Everyone at the table, including a new arrival or the shooter, can make a come bet on all subsequent tosses of the dice after the come-out roll. It's obvious that betting the come line before every roll of the dice can result in a very exciting and profitable situation if the dice stay away from 7. Of course, the 7 becomes a real threat after a number of come bets have been made, since it will wipe out the pass line as well as all the come bets. Even after the pass-line number is made, you are not looking for a natural 7 on a come-out roll, as it wipes out all the come bets in the number boxes, which we have learned can't be taken down. The dreaded 7 loses most of your bets, but it represents a winner on the final bet on the come line. Players frequently leave the table, forgetting this last winner. The house advantage on come bets is 1.41%, exactly the same as the pass-line bet.

I will offer several winning tips on how to use the come bet later in this chapter.

Don't Come

Don't-come wagers are the reverse of come bets and work the same as don't- pass-line bets. These wagers are positioned by the player in the space on the layout marked Don't Come Bar 12. The very next roll of the dice dictates the disposition of this bet. Craps 2 and 3 are winners and pay even money. Winnings are paid off on the don't-come bar, and if not picked up are added to the original bet, and the total becomes a new don't-come bet. As with the don't pass, 12 is a standoff and the bet can be canceled at the gambler's whim. A throw of 7 or 11 is a loser. Naturally, 4, 5, 6, 8, 9 or 10 becomes a don't come number, and the dealer will move the wager to your designated spot in the appropriate box on the layout. Again, the venturesome don't bettor may make a series of these bets, but unlike come bets, these wagers are lost one at a time if they are repeated before the seven is rolled. When the 7 is rolled, all don't come bets are won. The casino's edge on don't come is the same 1.40% as don't pass.

Place Bets

Place bets are by far the most popular number bets and resemble come bets in that you are betting on a particular number to be thrown before the 7. The difference is that your money goes right to the number instead of to the come line. Thus, if you put a bet on the table and announce to the dealer, "Place the 5," your chips are put on your designated spot in the place-5 box on the layout. If 5 is thrown before 7, you win and are paid off at 7-to-5 odds. The dealer will place your winnings in front of you and ask, "Same bet?" You can say, "Yes," and let the bet ride; or, "Take it down," and your bet will be returned; or, "Press it," and enough of your winnings will be taken to double your bet.

Your odds on this bet are not very good - the house advantage is 4%. If you place the 9, the house advantage is the same 4%. Placing the numbers 4 and 10 are even worse, yielding the casino 6.67%. A place bet on the 6 or 8 is a completely different matter; the casino advantage of 1.52% is just slightly more than the 1.41% for come bets.

Aggressive come bettors, eager for action, sometimes place the 6 and 8 right after the come-out roll, replacing the wager with a come bet if the number comes up. You must make place bets in increments of $6 to take full advantage of the odds when you place the 6 or 8. If you insist on placing 4, 5, 9 or 10, you must bet in increments of $5. If you bet less, you will be paid even money. If you bet more, you will be paid the odds on the next lower amount. Incidentally, place bettors of the 4 and 10 would reduce the casino's advantage from 6.67% to 4.76%, if they would buy instead of placing the bet. This requires betting in increments of $20 and is described in the next section.

Many craps players believe that place betting gives them a better deal, and the house less of an advantage, than come betting. This is not true. Come betting gives the house a small advantage of 1.41% as compared to place- betting advantages ranging from

1.52% to 6.67%. Why the large difference? Because when you make a come bet, you have a chance for an immediate winner when a natural 7 or 11 is thrown. It's true that you also lose immediately when craps 2, 3 or 12 is rolled, but this occurs only half as often.

Some players like to have all the numbers working for them immediately. $32 across the board," means place $5 on each of the numbers 4, 5, 9 and 10, and $6 on the 6 and 8. The 4 and 10 pay off at 9 to 5; the 5 and 9 pay off at 7 to 5; and the 6 and 8 pay off at 7 to 6. Thus, for every number the shooter rolls, the place bettor has a winner. The come bettor must wait for a number to be rolled twice before he can win - once to establish his point and the second time to win.

Place betting in this manner can be very dangerous to your bankroll. In addition to giving the casino a much higher advantage, five numbers must be rolled before you recoup your investment. A 7 thrown early in the series will wipe out your $32 bet with little, if any, return. I have seen many players walk up to a table and say, "$32 across the board," only to have a 7 on the very next roll wipe out their entire bet. In come betting, your entire investment is not risked all at once. Also, a 7-out early in the series is a winner for you; 7 is a winner for the last come bet.

Another argument that place bettors offer pertains to long runs. Most place bettors turn off their bets on the come-out roll. A place bet can be taken down at any time, and this is, essentially, what they are doing on the come-out roll. Thus, if the shooter throws a 7 on the come-out roll, the place bet is not lost. If their number is thrown, their bet isn't won either. The come bet can't be turned off on the come-out roll and is lost if a 7 pops up. The house caters to this superstition by automatically turning off all place bets on the come-out roll unless the dealer is specifically informed that the bets are working. The theory is that this is when the shooter is supposed to throw his 7's. Therefore, during a long run which includes some 7's on come-out rolls, the place bettor's progression keeps working, while the come bettor must start over again after the 7 is rolled. The smart craps player ignores this faulty reasoning, sticks to the pass line, and makes come bets to get on the numbers.

In my 30 + years of playing craps, most, if not all, of my really big scores have been with the come bet taking full odds. I really hope that my arguments in this section will make you a confirmed come better.

Buy Bets

Buy bets are nearly the same as place bets inasmuch as you are betting a given number will appear before a 7. The only difference is in the way the bet is made and the casino advantage. These bets are made by few craps players; in fact, I have never seen a buy bet on any number other than the 4 or 10. A

Place Bettor betting across the board will usually buy the 4 and 10 if he is betting in $25 units. It costs you 5% to buy either number and the minimum vigorish is $1 so it doesn't pay to buy the number for less than $20. The procedure is to toss the dealer a $25 chip plus a $1 chip (the "vig") and say: "I'm buying the 4 (or the 10)." The dealer puts the wager in your designated spot in the appropriate number box, and identifies it as a buy rather than a come bet with a small "buy" button placed on top of the stack of chips. If the number comes up, you win and are paid off at true odds, 2 to 1. The dealer tosses you $50 for your 2 to 1 payoff and says: "drop me a dollar" - the vig for the next bet. Just like place bets, buy bets are automatically off on come-out rolls and can be taken down at any time. If you elect to take down the buy bet, the 5% commission is returned to you.

Field Bets

A field bet, positioned by the player, is a one-roll bet. Unlike a pass-line bet, which occurs over a series of rolls, your field bet is won or lost on the next roll of the dice. This wager can be made at any time, and to the beginning craps player, the field bet appears to be a really good bet. After all, you've covered seven of the eleven numbers; 3, 4, 9, 10 and 11 pay even money and the 2 and 12 pay double. You lose only if the 5, 6, 7 or 8 comes up. However, if you examine the number of combinations in which each number can be rolled, it turns out you would lose 20 units and win 18 for every 36 units wagered. This equates to a casino advantage of over 5%. The field bet is definitely not a good bet to make. You are much better off sticking to the pass and come line, where the house advantage is only 1.41%.

Proposition Bets

"Five dollars on any craps. O. K. Who wants the eleven? Ten on the hard four." The stickman at the craps table is like a circus barker, standing in the center of the table and controlling the flow of the game. His primary job is to entice the players into making proposition bets. I call them sucker bets because the odds against you and in favor of the casino are extremely high: the casino edge ranges from 9.09 to 16.67%. Because of the extremely high odds against you, I am placing these bets outside the scope of this book; I do not recommend any of them. The only time you should even consider any of them is if you are winning big money and in the middle of a hot table. If you join *The Casino Gamblers' Network* and attend one of my Gambler's Clinics, ask me when I make these bets.

Also to be avoided are the Big Six and the Big Eight, prominently located in the corners of most payouts (no longer on the Atlantic City layout by state regulation). Big Six and/or Big Eight bets are positioned by the player, and win if the number appears before 7, paying even money. If you don't pick up your winnings and your original bet, it all rides on the next roll. The casino edge on this bet is a whopping 9.09%. If you want to bet on the 6 or 8, wager in multiples of $6 and "place" the number; then you will be paid at the rate of 7 to 6, decreasing the casino's advantage to 1.52%.

Free Odds

The first and foremost thing to remember is that this bet is paid at the correct odds; therefore, you have an even chance of winning. Thus, if the point number is 4 and the odds are taken, say, for $5, the house will pay $10 for winning this 2-to-1 wager. But stop! Don't get into the sedan or hop a bus just to take advantage of this. Remember, the house enjoys an edge on every play at the table. You can take advantage of the free-odds bet only if you have already made a wager on the pass line, don't pass, come, or don't come.

"Taking the odds," is the correct phrasing when a wager is made on the pass or come line. This bet is also known as a "right bet," and the player is, of course, a "right bettor." When a point is established - 4, 5, 6, 8, 9 or 10 - the bet is backed up by placing the odds wager directly behind the pass-line bet. Taking the odds on pass- and come-line bets reduces the casino advantage from 1.41 to 0.85%.

It is important to memorize the free odds so you can be paid off at the maximum rate. Backup bets on 5 and 9 should be made in increments of two, so the bet can be paid off at the rate of 3 to 2. The 6 and 8 should be backed up in increments of five, so the bet can be paid off at 6 to 5. The numbers 4 and 10 never become a problem, as the payoff rate is 2 to 1. In many casinos, your backup bet may not exceed the initial bet unless it's just a small increase to make your payoff come out even. For instance, if your pass-line bet is $4, your backup bet would be $4 if the come-out number is 5 or 9. With a come-out number of 6 or 8, the minimum backup bet to receive a 6-to-5 payoff would be $5.

The Free Odds bet is the most important on the layout and is central to all my advice on money management. Many craps authors advise always taking maximum odds. This is bad advice. It depends on your bankroll and we will get into the specifics of when and when not to take the odds later in this chapter. The other point I want to make on Free Odds right now is never, never lay the odds if you are playing the don't side. When the point is established, you have the advantage. Why give back part of it by laying the odds? There is also too much risk involved because you are always betting more than you are getting back.

How To Achieve The Winning Edge At Craps

My advice in this chapter is keyed to Do Side bettors. Don't Side bettors, pick up a copy of one of the many gaming books, choose a good betting progression and exercise patience. Or better yet, join *The Casino Gamblers' Network*^{tm} (see Chapter 12) because the method that comes with your membership, "Go With The Flow", starts with the Don't Side.

Tip 1: Find the hot table or be around when a table turns hot. Is this possible and if so, how? There is no mechanical formula, no cook book approach that I can give you. But I will say this and it's based on over 30 years of playing craps. Tables run in cycles - cold, choppy and hot. If you don't believe that, go out and observe 20 tables and you will know what I am talking about. The best way to pick a table is to avoid the obvious losing table where shooter after shooter establishes a point and then throws a very quick seven-out. Watch the dice and see how they're running. Are numbers coming up? How many before the seven-out? Notice the other players. Are they winning? Look at the layout. Is there money on come bets? On place bets? If your answers are coming up yes, this is your table.

Tip 2: Don't stay too long at any one table. If two or three players throw quick seven outs, you might be at the wrong table. Find another one using the criteria discussed above. Remember we are not discussing the mathematics of the craps table here; we are recognizing the realities of the game - that tables run in cycles and that your objective is to be there when the winning streak occurs. I would much rather risk my money at a table where the dice are passing (remember "passing" means that shooters are making their points) and the shooter is throwing numbers than hang around a cold table even if there is no mathematical basis for this decision.

In Chapter 3 on money management I recommend establishing a craps bankroll of 200 betting units; i.e. if you are playing with a $1000, your betting unit is 1000/200 (this is read 1000 divided by 200) or $5. And I recommend allocating 25% of this bankroll, or 50 units to your table play and as a table stop loss. Now I realize that smaller players may be establishing their craps bankroll without this much backing behind them so, for this discussion, let's assume you are walking up to the table with 50 units - either 50 $1 units; 50 $2 units ($100); or 50 $5 units ($250). Hopefully, you have another 150 units in reserve but, if not, the advice still applies. And if your unit size is $10 or higher, read on because this advice also applies to you.

A Progression Method Using The Odds Bet To Exploit Hot Tables

Here is the way you play. Play one unit on the pass line with no Free Odds bet. If you win this first bet, your next bet is one unit with a one unit odds bet rounded up depending on the number rolled. If your betting unit is $2, your odds bet is $2 for the 4,5,9,10 and $2.50 for the 6 and 8 (Nevada 25 cent tables only).

If your betting unit is $3, your odds bet is $3 for the 4 and 10, $4 for the 5 and 9 and $5 for the 6 and 8.

If you win this second bet, you continue to bet one unit on the pass line but now will risk two units on your odds bet - double your pass line bet (assuming the casino allows double odds, which most do).

You do not increase your pass line bet until you have won three bets - one with no odds, one with single odds and one with double odds - then you increase your pass line bet to two units. On your first bet at two units you take single odds. If you win you stay at two units but with double odds. On the next win progress to four units, single odds; then four units double odds. And so on. Here is a picture of how your betting pattern would increase on successive wins:

First bet: 1 unit; **Second bet**: 1 unit with 1 unit odds bet; **Third bet**: 1 unit with 2 unit odds bet; **Fourth bet**: 2 units with 2 units odds bet; **Fifth bet**: 2 units with 4 units odds bet; **Sixth bet**: 4 units with 4 units odds bet; **Seventh bet**: 4 units with 8 units odds bet; **Eighth bet**: 8 units with 8 unit odds bet; **Ninth bet**: 8 units with 16 units odds bet.

Of course your odds bet should be rounded up to a multiple of 5 if your point is six or eight.

Keep progressing but only on successive wins and progress until you lose; then return to a one unit bet.

If your casino offers triple odds or higher, use a similar progression pattern incorporating the triple odds, i.e. bet 2,2; 2,4; 2,6 before progressing to 3 units.

ANY TIME YOU LOSE YOU BACK OFF TO A ONE UNIT BET AND START THE ENTIRE PROGRESSION OVER AGAIN.

This method is absolutely the soundest advice you will get anywhere for minimizing your risk while allowing you to participate in a hot table with a short bankroll. You <u>can</u> bet more aggressively, but, if you do, you are increasing your risk to intolerable levels and jeopardizing your bankroll.

How To Incorporate Come Bets Into Your Betting Progression

You can use this method for come bets in a similar way. You make a total of three come bets only. You must win three come bets on any one shooter before you start the progression described above. Do not progress to the next level until you have won three bets at the prior level. Example: you make three come bets of one unit each. You win any three come bets. On the third win, your next bet is now one unit with a one unit odds bet. As each winning come bet, without odds, comes down, you replace it with one with odds until you have a total of three come bets with one unit of odds. After you have won a total of three come bets with a one unit odds bet, your next bet is one unit but with a two unit odds bet. Continue in a similar manner until the shooter sevens out.

What do you do with your come bets on the come out roll? First of all, you let all of your odds bets "work." You must tell this to the dealer because, otherwise, your odds are always off on the come out. You do this because the come out roll is no different than any other roll and you want your odds bets working at all times for maximum return. If the shooter throws a seven wiping out your come bets, go back to betting one unit with the odds and continue from there.

The craps method I will send you if you join *The Casino Gamblers' Network*[tm] is a little bit different than this money management technique. It is a method for going with the flow of the table and betting either pass or don't pass. Table selection is not as important because you are looking for winning opportunities on the don't side while waiting for a hot table to develop.

Summary Of Winning Tips And Ideas

- Avoid the proposition bets and the field bet.

- Your chances of achieving a big win on a long roll are much higher by playing come bets and taking full odds than by making place bets. A come bet strategy is recommended.

- Use some discretion in selecting your table. Look for a winning table with chips in the players' trays and on the betting layout.

- Do not stay at any one table too long. The dice do run in cycles and, even though there is no mathematical proof, it doesn't hurt to look for another table where the numbers are going your way.

- Let the table prove itself before investing in the Free Odds bet. Even though the odds bet reduces the house advantage, it does increase your risk so the correct approach is to use a progression betting method for the pass line and come, in which you phase into using the odds bet on successive wins. (Details in chapter.)

CHAPTER 8: HOW TO PLAY AND WIN AT ROULETTE

To the novice player, the betting layout for roulette looks formidable, but the game is really quite easy to learn. The main section is composed of 36 red and black boxes numbered in sequence from top to bottom and arranged in three columns of 12 boxes each. At the head of the columns, number 1, 2 and 3, are two more oddly shaped green spaces for the zeros. At the foot of these columns are three spaces marked "2 to 1." A bet placed in one of these indicates that you are betting on all the numbers in the column above. Directly along the front side of the columns are three boxes marked "1st 12", "2nd 12", and "3rd 12." A bet placed in the first of these indicates you are betting on all the numbers 1 through 12, a bet in the second would cover 13 through 24, and in the third it would cover 25 through 36. Just in front of these three are six more spots for wagers on numbers 1 through 18, for wagers on all even numbers, for wagers on all red spots, for wagers on all black spots, for wagers on all odd numbers, and for wagers on the numbers 19 through 36. You must be careful that your chips are placed precisely where you want to bet. If you can't reach a spot, slide your chips toward the dealer and tell him where to place them.

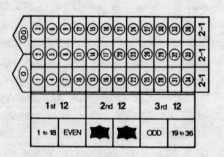

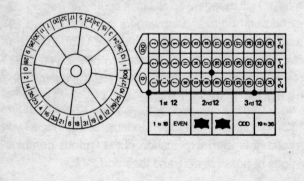

Roulette Wheel

The game of roulette is based on a random choice of one of 38 numbers selected through the use of a wheel made up of a stationary 32-inch bowl which contains a precisely balanced rotating 24-inch center section called a wheel head. A steel ball is spun by the dealer in a clockwise direction around the outer rim of the bowl, and after circling a number of times, the whirling ball slowly drops down toward the center, frequently being randomly deflected by brass projections embedded in the rim. As it reaches the wheel head, which is turning in the opposite direction, the ball bounces around a number of times among the vertical partitions that separate the 38 numbered red, black and green pockets before it finally settles in one of them, thereby selecting the winning number and color.

The 38 pockets, which are alternately colored red and black except for the green zeros, appear to be numbered in a random fashion, but that is not the case. As far as possible, high and low as well as odd and even numbers are alternately spaced in a mathematically balanced pattern. The single zero and the double zero are directly opposite each other, and 1 is opposite 2, 3 is opposite 4 and so forth. The numbers and colors on the wheel correspond to the numbers and colors on the layout. Understanding this, all you need now is an explanation of the various combinations of possible bets and their odds.

With only eleven possible wagers divided into just two types, betting rules are easily learned. First, let's consider the six inside bets on the numbers or combinations of numbers.

Types Of Bets

To make the single-number inside bet (called **"straight up"**), simply place your chips in any one of the 38 number boxes, including the zeros, being careful that your bet does not touch any line. If the ball lands in the corresponding numbered pocket on the next spin, you win and the bank pays off at 35 to 1. Remember that your original bet stays on the layout and rides on the next spin unless you pick it up. True odds would have been 37 to 1; consequently, the house advantage is 5.26%. This edge is constant for all bets in the double-zero game, with the exception of the five-number bet covered below. When you find a single-zero game, the casino edge is reduced to 2.70%.

If you want to bet on either of two adjoining numbers on the layout (called a **"split bet"**), put your wager directly on the line separating them. If one of them wins, you are paid off at 17 to 1. There are 62 possible two-number bets.

For a **three-number bet,** set your chip or chips on the line at the end of any of the twelve rows of three numbers; at the junction of the 0, 00 and 2 boxes; the 0, 1 and 2 boxes; or the 00, 2 and 3 boxes. This adds up to fifteen available three-number bets, and the payoff is 11 to 1.

A chip placed at the intersection of any four numbers is called a **corner bet**. There are 22 of these, and if any one of the four numbers comes up, you are paid 8 to 1.

The only possible **five-number bet** is on the line between the zeros and 1, 2 and 3 at the intersection with the 1st-12 box. Of course, this bet is not available in a single-zero game. In the double-zero game, it's the worst bet on the table, paying 6 to 1, with the casino advantage jumping to 7.89%.

You can make a **six-number bet** on the junction formed by the line dividing any two rows of three numbers where it intersects with the Dozen box. The bank pays 5 to 1 if you bet on one of these eleven combinations and any one of the six numbers is spun.

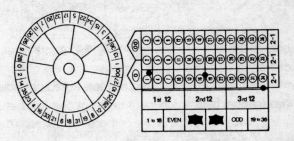

Next we'll explore the five outside bets, covering several groups of numbers, even-odd, and red-black, all spread over twelve betting boxes. These wagers still carry the same house edge of 5.26% for the double-zero game, and your original bet still is left on the layout after a win.

When you place a bet in one of the three boxes at the bottom of the number columns, you are making a **column bet** and betting on all the numbers above it; if successful, you'll be paid at the 2-to-1 rate printed in these spots.

To wager on the first, second and third **dozen** numbers, put your chips in one of the appropriate boxes. If any one of the twelve numbers within the dozen you've selected shows up, the bank also pays 2 to 1.

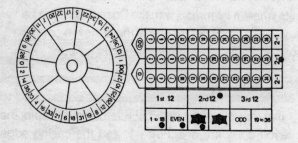

For a bet on all the eighteen low numbers or all the eighteen high numbers (a **high bet** or a **low bet**), merely set some chips in one of these two boxes. You will get even money if you win.

Chips placed in either the **even** or the **odd** box cover all the eighteen corresponding numbers, and winners are again paid even money.

To make a bet on all the **red** or **black** numbers, set some chips in the designated box for another possible even-money payoff.

The Atlantic casinos offer a very favorable rule to the player on the outside bets: even/odd, red/black, high/low. If a single zero or double zero is rolled, the player loses only half the bet. This is called "surrender" as the player surrenders half his bet on these situations. This favorable rule only pertains to the outside numbers and cuts the casinos advantage in half for outside bets - from 5.26% to 2.13%.

Casino Advantage

The mathematics of roulette are easily learned. On the double-zero wheel with 38 positions, the player should be able to pick the winning number an average of once every 38 spins. Although the odds are 37 to 1 that you will select the right number in one spin, the payoff odds are only 35 to 1, and the casino edge derived from this difference of two units is 5.26%.

Learning The Hard Way

I remember my first trip to Las Vegas. Fresh out of college and armed with an "unbeatable" roulette system, I came to conquer the casinos. I didn't care about the casinos' 5.26% advantage because, with my betting strategy, I knew I could overcome it. I was using a Martingale System and betting exclusively on red. Martingale System rules involved doubling the bet size on losses to the point where the next win would yield a one-unit profit. (The term "Martingale" originated from a London casino operator of the eighteenth century named Henry Martingale, who was always encouraging his patrons to "double up and catch up.") The first day, all went according to plan. The system was working beautifully. At one point, I had almost doubled my $100 bankroll. Then I hit a string of losses. My system was based on the fact that I would not lose nine times in succession. The odds against this were one in 512, so I figured I was safe. If it did happen, however, I was wiped out.

I sat at the table and watched black come up five times in a row. I dutifully increased my bet on red. Black again. By this time I was very nervous but I still bet red according to the system rules. The croupier spun the ball; mentally, I was trying to influence the outcome by "willing" red to occur. Black again. Now beads of sweat were breaking out on my forehead, but I was bound and determined to see this thing through. I pushed almost half of my remaining chips to the red. To no avail. It was almost as if fate was conspiring against me. Now all my chips were on the table. By this time I had lost all of my confidence and I knew I was going to lose. I did.

The train ride back to Los Angeles was long and filled with hunger pangs. I had even lost my dinner money. This loss cooled my ardor for the game for many years and is one of the main reasons I discovered blackjack and learned that the player could gain an advantage at the blackjack tables. Years later my interest in roulette was re-ignited when I met Scott Lang. Scott discovered a method for timing the wheel and predicting the sector into which the ball would fall. But that's another story that I don't have the space to tell you here. (Ask me at a Gamblers' Clinic.)

How To Achieve The Winner's Edge At Roulette

I suggest sticking to the outside bets especially in Atlantic City where the Surrender option halves the house advantage.

When in Nevada try to find single-zero wheels; they do pop up from time to time and halve the house advantage against you. This can affect your results even in the short-term as you wait for the outcomes that will make you a winner.

I would not employ any betting progression method which involves betting up on losses at a $5 or higher minimum table. Demand a $1 minimum table and establish your betting unit as $1. $1 tables are common in Nevada but much more difficult to find in Atlantic City where the casinos must maintain higher win rates to pay their higher expenses. I must caution you that this advice usually conflicts with my advice of finding a single-zero wheel; if you find one they usually offer a much higher minimum bet, in some cases $25. If you choose to play with a $5 or higher betting unit, play a betting progression like the "Reverse La Bouchere" that involves progressing on a win and not on a loss (described in Norman Leigh's *Thirteen Against The Bank*). If you are progressing your bet on losses, I recommend keeping your betting level to the $1 minimum or even lower as you can in some Nevada casinos. This is the preferred unit for the progression betting method to be discussed next.

The Rouge Et Colonne (Red & Column) Method

There are three columns of numbers on the roulette wheel and they extend, horizontally, in front of you as you face the layout. Each column contains 12 numbers and, since there is about one chance in three of each column hitting (excluding consideration of the two green zeros), the house payoff is 2 to 1. That is, if you bet $1 on a column and one of its numbers hits, you win $2 and get back a total of $3 including your $1 bet.

The middle column contains eight black and four red numbers. There are ten black and fourteen red numbers dispersed among the other two columns.

The essence of our strategy is betting one unit on the even-money red and one unit on the middle column as a hedge against a black number showing up. Since this middle column contains more black numbers than either of the other two columns, there is a better chance that if a black number is rolled, it will be in the middle column.

Here are the four possible outcomes of betting in this fashion:

1. A red number is rolled in the middle column: We win one unit on red and two units on the middle column for a total win of three units;

2. A red number is rolled in either columns 1 or 3: We win one unit on red and lose one unit on the middle column for a wash;

3. A black number is rolled in the middle column: We lose one unit on red and win two units on the middle column for a total win of one unit;

4. A black number is rolled in either columns 1 or 3: We lose one unit on red and lose one unit on the middle column for a total loss of two units.

If you tally up the various wins and losses, you will see that out of 37 typical spins on a single-zero wheel, you win 12 and lose 11; out of 38 typical spins on a double-zero wheel, you win 12 times and lose 12 times.

But don't think you have been given the keys to the casino cage. We are still bucking a house advantage of 5.26% with two zeros and 2.13% with one

(2.13% in Atlantic City with the half loss on even money bets.) The secret to your success with this method is to learn a negative progression. It is structured to win the larger bets and lose the smaller ones. You bet up on a loss; down on a win. The key to our success is the unlikelihood of running into a long series of consecutive losses due to the effect of the red bet in the first and third columns. It is not uncommon to be out of the middle column for ten straight spins but most of these should be red, resulting in a tie.

Another factor in our success is strict adherence to the money management rules. Betting up on successive losses, we go back one level on a win through the third level and, beyond that - the fourth level and above - we retreat two levels on a win. Here is the negative progression (betting up on successive losses) and betting the same amount on red and the middle column: 1, 2, 3, 5, 7, 9, 12, 15, 18, 22.

The total bank required under the worst case scenario is 188 units.

Example: If you lost the first four bets and are now up to the seven-unit bet and you win, your next bet is three units on the red and three units on the middle column ((because you retreat two levels). If we encounter an uncommon amount of losses, retreating two levels on a win is our means of capital preservation. Naturally, luck will be a factor, as a win on red in the middle column at a high bet level will wipe out much of our previous losses. But on the other hand, that is one of the advantages of the Rouge Et Colonne Method.

Obviously, Rouge Et Colonne is a grind type of play, but isn't the casino structured to grind you out of your money? Our strategy does not call for betting up on successive wins. We are content to grind out the single unit wins, exposing a minimum of our bankroll. We recommend stopping play after winning 30% to 40% of your buy-in. Many times after achieving 30% win, you will win several bets in succession. Cash in after your first loss. A loss of a playing bankroll requires about three wins in subsequent sessions to get our money back.

I suggest practicing with $1 units or even less if you are playing in Nevada. In Nevada, you have a smaller house advantage at single-zero wheels (a few of which can still be found). In Atlantic City, you have the advantage of losing only half your even money bet when the green zeros come up (because of surrender). This, effectively, cuts the casino odds to 2.13% for even money bets - the same as a single-zero wheel.

There are methods that have been developed for beating the wheel, such as Scott Lang's Target Sectoring mentioned above, but they are beyond the scope of this book. When you attend one of my Casino Gambler's Clinics as part of your Gamblers'

Network membership, be sure to ask me about clocking the wheel and clocking the dealer.

Summary Of Winning Tips And Ideas

- Stick to the even-money bets in Atlantic City where the house advantage is half of all other bets.

- When in Nevada try to find single-zero wheels which also cuts the house advantage in half.

- When using a betting progression on losses, use a $1 betting unit. The Rouge Et Colonne Method is recommended.

- If your betting unit is $5 or higher, use a progression on successive wins, such as the Reverse La Bouchere.

CHAPTER 9: HOW TO PLAY AND WIN AT BACCARAT

Kidney-shaped to allow room for the dealers to reach out and handle both the bets and the cards, the baccarat table itself is about twelve feet long and three to four feet wide. The green baize covering is stenciled with a baccarat layout providing numbered boxes in front of each chair for players to wager on either the banker or player hand. The places are numbered from one to fifteen, with thirteen omitted, as few gamblers would be willing to sit and play at that traditionally unlucky spot.

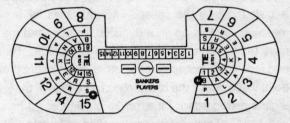

The modern version of the ancient game of baccarat is played with eight decks, shuffled by the caller, cut by a player, and placed in a dealing box called a shoe, after the insertion of a cut card near the end of the combined decks to indicate the last hand. The shoe is then passed to a player at seat number one, who becomes the banker, although he may bet either hand. The shoe moves counterclockwise around the table each time the bank hand loses. Any player who becomes the banker may elect to pass the bank, then or at the completion of any hand, but to be eligible to deal, the banker must have at least a minimum bet on the table in either position.

After all wagers are placed, the banker alternately deals out four cards, face down, first to the caller, who slides two cards to a player (traditionally the largest bettor for that hand), and two to himself, sliding these banker's cards under a corner of the shoe. The player then turns over his two cards and tosses them to the caller, who announces the total. Following this, the banker uncovers the two cards that were tucked under the corner of the shoe, and their value is called out by the caller. The four suits have no meaning. At this point, a decision for the hand may have been reached with just these four cards. Tens and face cards count zero; all other cards count their point value; and if the hand totals more than 9, the left digit is disregarded; thus, unlike blackjack, no hand can bust. Totals of 8 or 9, called "naturals," are automatic winners, although of course a natural 9 beats a natural 8. If the player hand adds up to 6, 7, 8 or 9, or if the banker hand totals 7, 8 or 9, no additional cards are dealt and the hand that comes closest to a total of 9 wins and all bets are settled. Ties are a push; no money is exchanged and players are free to change their bets as they choose.

Frequently, the totals of two hands require a third card to be dealt to the player, the banker, or both.

Neither one has a choice in the matter - the rules are fixed. Optimal strategy has been developed for every possible combination of cards, and since as many as fifteen players are wagering on just two hands, to avoid arguments over poor play, standing and drawing decisions are mandatory. Remember, though, neither player nor banker ever draws against a natural 8 or 9.

Rules For Player's Hand

If the rules require the player to stand on his initial two cards, the caller announces, "Player stands with [point total]." But if the player must draw, the croupier calls, "Card for the player." Only then does the banker deal a card face up to the croupier, who places it next to the first two cards as he announces the new total. The decisions for the player's hand are easy to learn. If the initial cards total 5 or less, draw one and only one card; otherwise, stand. When the player's hand is completed, the procedure for completing the banker's hand is the same, but the rules for drawing or standing are a little more complicated.

Rules For Banker's Hand

Except for initial cards totaling 2 or less, which always require a draw, the decisions for the banker's hand vary depending on the player's third card. Again, only one card may be drawn, and it's always taken if the banker's hand totals:

3 and the player stands or draws 1, 2, 3, 4, 5, 6, 7, 9 or 10.

4 and the player stands or draws 2, 3, 4, 5, 6 or 7.

5 and the player stands or draws 4, 5, 6 or 7.

6 and the player draws 6 or 7. The dealer must stand if the player stands.

These rules are summarized in the boxes below.

PLAYER RULES

HAVING	
1-2-3-4-5-10	DRAWS A CARD
6-7	STANDS
8-9	NATURAL Bank cannot draw.

BANK RULES

HAVING	DRAWS WHEN GIVING	DOES NOT DRAW WHEN GIVING
3	1-2-3-4-5-6-7-9-10	8
4	2-3-4-5-6-7	1-8-9-10
5	4-5-6-7	1-2-3-8-9-10
6	6-7	1-2-3-4-5-8-9-10
7	STANDS	
8-9	NATURAL Player cannot draw.	

Notice that the rules can require the banker to draw even when his first two cards beat the player's final hand, and a third card can cause the banker's hand to lose. When both hands are concluded, the caller declares the winner, announcing the point total for each.

Because the inherent odds of the game favor the banker over the player, the casinos assess a 5% commission on all winning bets on the banker so that the house advantage on either hand is about the same, 1.06% on the banker vs. 1.23% on the player. The casino pays even money on all bets, which amounts to an overpayment on winning banker bets, but you don't have to worry about keeping track of the commissions on these bets; the dealers do this for you with tokens that are placed in your numbered commission box in front of them, each time you bet and win on the banker's hand. The accumulated commissions are collected by the dealers while the cards are being shuffled for the next round, and they must be paid before you leave the table if you quit during a shoe. Always be aware of your commission indebtedness, and never bet your last chips before settling up.

The Streak

Mr. K. is a high roller. There is no doubt about it. I got to know him when he called me about participating in my Blackjack Clinic. He told me that he had dropped $25,000 playing baccarat and he wanted to find a way to win it back. I told him that I could teach him how to win at blackjack, but that I couldn't guarantee how much he'd win.

Mr. K. took the Blackjack Clinic and became an excellent and disciplined blackjack player. Or so I thought. It turns out that he did win back his $25,000, although it wasn't just because of the advantage that I had taught him how to achieve at blackjack. He had a series of very lucky sessions where all the cards were going his way. I told Mr. K. not to count on the same heavy winnings in every session and sure enough, his luck turned - he dropped about $10,000. At that point, he returned to baccarat. He got lucky again and won back his $10,000 and then began alternating his play between blackjack and baccarat. Although he still plays an excellent game of blackjack, Mr. K. is a gambler - he possesses the gambler's urgency to play for high stakes. He seeks, as all true gamblers do, an "adrenalin high."

One day Mr. K. invited me down to observe his play at the baccarat tables. Agreeing to meet him in front of the baccarat pit prior to starting play, I arrived at the appointed time, only to find Mr. K. already in the game, looking very distressed. He had arrived two days earlier and was down about $10,000. Mr. K. expressed the usual gambler's lament about not quitting when he was ahead; at one point he had been up $5,000.

I sat down to play alongside Mr. K. Down to his last $500, he had used up his $4,000 credit line, so there was nothing he could do if he dropped that last

$500. I watched it dwindle down to $50 and then talked him into having lunch.

During lunch, I attempted to talk Mr. K. into going home, licking his wounds, and returning another day to play blackjack, where he could enjoy a positive advantage instead of the negative one-plus percent at baccarat, but to no avail. In fact, he talked me into cashing a check for him for $1,000. I agreed on the condition that we would play blackjack. O. K. But we couldn't find a seat! Not even at a $25 table.

Mr. K. suggested baccarat. I reluctantly acquiesced. One table was full and one table was empty. Mr. K. chose the empty table with the exclamation, "Let it [the recoup or the wipeout] happen fast!"

Now, Mr. K. is a streak bettor, looking for a long series of wins in a row on either the bank or the players. He bets whatever has come up last until it loses. For example, if the bank wins, he keeps betting the bank until the players win. Then he jumps to the players until the bank wins, and so on.

Well, it was Mr. K.'s lucky day, because we caught a shoe with a lot of streaks, starting with 16 straight wins for the players. Mr. K.'s betting progressed from $40 to $500. As I was willing to risk only $100, my betting progressed from $20 to $200 in a conservative progression as follows: 20-20-40-40-60-60-80-100-120-140-160-180-200.

This is one of the most amazing streaks I had ever seen in my twenty-two years of playing casino games. The odds of getting a group of sixteen wins in a row are about 65,000 to one. During the streak, there were certain things prescribed by Mr. K. to keep it going: the player's cards were turned over by the same person each time; the banker's cards were always tapped against Mr. K.'s chips; the only conversation allowed was in conjunction with the bet size; and counting chips was prohibited. But this streak was not the last good thing to come out of this fantastic shoe; three or four other streaks of five or six wins occurred, and at the end of the shoe, Mr. K. had recouped his $10,000 and had won another $1,000 to boot. I had multiplied my $100 by sixteen. Our play had begun at 3:00 PM and at 4:03 PM, we were cashing in at the cashier's cage.

There is no moral to this story, but I will give you some advice on baccarat. If you're feeling lucky, set aside part of your casino bankroll for a fling at the baccarat tables. And if you do play baccarat, use Mr. K.'s method. Maybe you'll catch a streak.

CHAPTER 10: HOW TO WIN AT VIDEO POKER

When you sit down to play at a video poker machine you are playing what is fast becoming the most popular Slot Machine in the country. Huge billboards on the Ben Franklin Bridge leading from Philadelphia to the Atlantic City Expressway loudly advertise the video poker machines of the Atlantic City casinos. In Nevada when you go into many bars you can drink free ... as long as you are feeding dollars into the video poker machines which line the top of the bar from one end to the other. In Montana, a state with only legalized poker, there are 50,000 video poker machines.

Why the popularity?

Because skill is involved. Gamblers are getting bored with sitting at regular slot machines and pulling the handle hour after hour. In Video Poker there are decisions to make; you are involved! And the odds of winning expressed by the pay off scale, are readily apparent. There is also the thrill of going for the royal flush with it's 4000 coin payoff (or progressive jackpot).

So if you are a slot player and haven't tried video poker, you're missing a lot of fun - not to mention better winning odds than on most regular slot machines.

Video Poker is easy to play even if you know nothing about poker; you can sit down at any machine and examine the pay off table to get the idea. The pay off table shows you the hierarchy of winning hands and related pay offs (listed from lowest pay off to highest pay off): Jacks or better; 2 pair; 3 of a kind; straight; flush; full house; 4 of a kind; straight flush and royal flush.

If you are a poker player, all of the above terms make sense to you and you can jump ahead and read my winning tips.

If you are unfamiliar with some of these pay off terms, here is a simple explanation. Jacks or better means a pair of jacks, queens, kings or aces. A pair of 10s or lower does not pay off. Two pair means just what it says: two of any pair such as a pair of sevens and a pair of fours. Three of a kind is a little harder to draw and thus pays more than two pair. A Straight is five cards in succession such as 2, 3, 4, 5, 6. Or 10, J, Q, K, Ace. The ace can count either high or low in your sequence. A flush is five cards of the same suit such as five diamonds. Sequence is not involved as it is with a straight. A full house is three of a kind and a pair such as 3 fives and 2 Aces. Four of a kind is just what it says. A straight flush is a straight in the same suit; very difficult to draw, that's why the high pay off. A Royal Flush is the very top hand: 10, J, Q, K, Ace in the same suit.

Your decisions are what make the game so interesting. You have to decide what hand you are shooting for. Naturally the higher the hand, the higher the pay off. And you have to decide when to go for the royal flush and capture the 4000 coin pay off. Here are some tips that give you a better chance of winning and definitely cut your losses down.

Whenever possible play only machines that offer Jacks or better on their pay off line. If a casino doesn't pay off on Jacks or better, try to find one that does.

Sometimes you are confronted by a decison to play in a casino offering 2 pair as a minimum payoff but with a progressive jackpot versus a casino that pays on Jacks or better but with no progressive jackpot. In general, you are still better off playing the Jacks or better.

However, if there is a progressive jackpot on the 2 pair machine paying twice as much as a 4000 coin pay off, choose the 2 pair machine. For example, in The Claridge recently, there was a progressive jackpot of over $2300 on a quarter machine. Now 4000 coins is just $1000 so you are better off opting for the big progressive jackpot.

To get the 4000 coin pay off for the Royal Flush, you must play five coins. This is a given. If you play the game, play the five coins. If you are reluctant to play five dollars a pop on a $1 machine, find the quarter machines; many casinos have them.

Check the pay offs carefully because some casinos pay more for certain hands than others. Get into the habit of writing down the pay off line and then comparison shopping for a better line in other casinos. Here are the typical pay offs from two casinos in Atlantic City both paying on Jacks or better. Which would you choose? (Pay offs shown are for a five coin play).

Royal Flush:	4000	4000
Straight Flush:	250	250
4 of a kind:	125	100
Full House:	35	35
Flush:	25	25
Straight:	20	20
3 of a kind:	15	15
2 pair:	10	10
Jacks or better:	5	5

It is obvious that you would play in the casino offering a 125 coin pay off on 4 of a kind.

The above are typical payoffs; you can do better if you shop around.

If you get paid on Jacks or better, these pay offs are usually less than a casino that does not pay off on Jacks or better. In this case accept the lower pay offs and take the Jacks or better; your odds of winning are better. The idea is to stay in the game longer waiting for the Royal Flush and you can do that with the many even pay offs of the Jacks or better.

Look for machines with a progressive jackpot on the Royal Flush. If the dollar amount is greater than 4000 coins, this is the machine you want to play. For example if you see a progressive jackpot on a quarter machine totaling $1330 why would you play a machine paying only 4000 coins or $1000? (except for the Jacks or better versus 2 pair decision discussed above).

When you play the hands, be aggressive in going for a Royal Flush. Draw two cards to a potential Royal Flush as long as it doesn't break up a winning hand. If you have a four card Royal Flush with any pair, break up the pair and go for the Royal Flush even if it's a winning pair.

If you have a hand containing a pair, don't keep a kicker; draw three cards to go for the three of a kind or better.

Check your hands carefully for the possibility of a straight. With the cards appearing at random in the windows, sometimes it is overlooked.

If you are considering drawing to an inside straight, i.e. 2, 3, 10, 5, 6 (you're throwing away the 10 and hoping to catch the 4), don't do it if you have a Jack or higher - go for the Jacks or better (assuming the machine pays off on Jacks or better).

Be wary of playing machines which feature a "joker." The pay offs on these machines are much less than on machines with no joker. You are usually better off playing the machines with the higher pay offs.

Try to play the casinos where the video poker machines are clustered in one location. This makes it much easier to compare the pay offs with the casino up the street.

One final tip. Check out *The Casino Gamblers Network*[tm] described in Chapter 12. One of the services is a Gamblers' Hotline which keeps you posted on the casinos offering the best video poker games including those that pay a jackpot on the royal flush.

What is the best Video Poker game? Look for these three factors: (1) Pays on Jacks or better; (2) A progressive jackpot value greater than 4000 coins, (3) Pays 30 to 5 on a flush and 45 to 5 on a full house (instead of the usual 25 and 35 respectively). If you find a game with these three factors, you may have an advantage over the casino (depending on your level of skill in playing the hands.)

CHAPTER 11: HOW TO DEVELOP AND USE SELF-CONTROL TO MAINTAIN YOUR WINNING EDGE

In my 12 + years of teaching I have never failed to offer instruction on money management in the home study course or classroom. I have taught my students how to establish a bankroll and how to bet in relation to their bankroll. Many of them listened to me, practiced their betting procedure and then went to the casino and did something entirely different. Why? I kept asking myself. I knew what they were doing because they called me up to discuss why they lost.

The problems always boiled down to a lack of mental preparation, to the student's inability to operate in a casino environment. Let's face it. When you walk into a casino, they want you to play on their terms, not yours. That's why they bombard you with free drinks, loud music, myriad colors and a free and easy atmosphere. That's why you play with chips and not money. After all what's a chip but a piece of plastic? Most gamblers are mesmerized by the typical casino environment and lose all self-control. If they had any kind of game plan at all they quickly forget it in the excitement of the action. If they lose, they roll a credit card and get more money.

I began to realize that there was a missing link in my instructions to my students on how to exercise self-control and mental discipline. I instituted instruction on mental discipline in 1982 with the help of a Southern California hypnotist. He attended one of my classes and we collaborated on using self hypnosis techniques prior to a casino trip or session. I noticed better results immediately.

In 1983 I was the recipient of a one-year research program which resulted in Eddie Olsen's *Successful Gambler Program*. Eddie's research looked at all of the self-improvement techniques on the market and incorporated the best of them into the *Successful Gambler Program*. This course represented breakthrough thinking in the field of gambling instruction and was and still is a major factor in the success of my Blackjack Home Study Course featuring the TARGET Method.

In 1988 I was the recipient of another breakthrough - from a very well known southern California psychologist who treats many movie stars. He also just happens to be one of my most successful students. His technique involves the manipulation of mental image pictures and can be done anywhere - at home or in the casino.

This technique is so powerful that I arranged to have this person attend all of my classroom instruction programs. He works both with groups and with each student on an individual basis.

What all of this research, development and application has taught me is one very important fact which is one of the major reasons I wrote this book. *Mental preparation and self-control are 90% of your winning edge!* You can learn the fundamentals of the games and how to bet but if you are not mentally ready to play, your level of risk is just too high.

You've got to realize that many mistakes inside the casinos are the consequences of problems outside the casino. Understanding and dealing with this relationship is very important on your road to becoming a winner.

Think back. How many times have you felt mesmerized and totally out of control, pulling more money out of your pocket without wanting to, staying at tables longer than you know you should, playing too many tables and losing more than you planned to lose? These are the problems that you've got to deal with before you can start winning on a consistent basis.

The bottom line is not just how much you take off the table, it is how much you don't lose, how much you don't give away to the casino. This aspect of your game plan is just as important as your winning tables. How many times has a big win been nullified by unnecessary losses? This is another example of a problem that must be addressed before we get into the technical skill areas.

Because of proprietary considerations and legal agreements with my associates, I cannot disclose all of the details of these mental conditioning techniques. BUT I CAN GET YOU STARTED! And if I do nothing more than convince you of their importance, I will have fullfilled my purpose in writing this book.

Let me give you a framework for managing your emotions and your time and accomplishing proper mental preparation for each casino trip and session. It is comprised of the following five steps:

- Establishing Goals and Objectives

- Developing And Documenting A Game Plan

- Visualizing Goals And Objectives

- Execution Of The Plan

- Monitoring And Evaluating The Plan

Now let's discuss each of these steps.

Step 1: Establishing Goals And Objectives

First answer the question: why am I gambling? For fun? To get away once in a while from a stressful environment? To feel the rush of an adrenalin high? To make money and win on a consistent basis? To make a living? Most people gamble for fun and enjoyment but others are more serious about the games. After you answer this question you can decide what you want to accomplish; what goals you want to realize.

For example if you wish to gamble to win on a consistent basis or to make a living you should choose blackjack as your primary game because you can gain an advantage over the casino.

If you're gambling for fun, you have to decide on whether or not you want the action or the money. For example if you establish the goal of doubling your bankroll on a weekend's play, what do you do if you accomplish this on Saturday and you still have plenty of time left before the weekend is over? You need to think about and write down these overall goals and objectives.

Many high rollers are happy to break even and that is their goal. They get the thrill and glamour of the casino, everything they want for free and if they play smart, it doesn't cost them a dime.

Let me suggest a goal to you. Build a bankroll. How much money are you playing with now? $500? $1000? Why not establish a goal of building a gambling bankroll of $5000 or $10,000? Then you can live like a king or queen and let the casinos pick up the tab for all your expenses (which they are perfectly willing to do). There is an interesting case study about one of our students starting our with just a $100 bankroll, playing only dealer-breaking tables, and going on to build a bankroll and then win $75,000 in his second year of play? This student established a very strong goal and directed all of his blackjack activities, including practice and play, to the accomplishment of this goal. He also followed steps 2 through 5 below.

Step 2: Develop And Document A Game Plan

Write down your goals and how you intend to accomplish them. Decide which games you are going to focus on and how often you intend to visit the casinos. Decide on how much money will be in your initial bankroll. Pick up a spiral bound notebook at the drug store and hand-write a page or two. Here is an outline of what to cover:

- goals and objectives

- schedule of casino visits

- Games you intend to learn well (e.g. black-jack)

- schedule and drills for home practice

- money management parameters (see Chapter 3 for specifics)

- Typical trip plan including trip duration, casinos to play, session schedule

You will be surprised at the satisfaction you will derive from this simple exercise of writing these items on a page or two of paper.

Step 3: Practice Visualization Of Goals And Objectives

If you have ever read a self improvement book you will understand what this is all about. You are asked to visualize in your mind what it is you intend to accomplish. And you are asked to do this on a daily basis, or even a few times during the day. Many successful people attrlbute their success to visualization techniques. Properly used they can help anyone and especially the casino gambler.

Here are a few tips to get you started. Visualize an event that can realistically happen. For example, do not visualize winning $100,000 at the craps table because there is very little chance that can happen. Make a specific goal such as adhering to a stop loss. Suppose your session stop loss is $100 and your objective is to take a one hour break if you hit that stop loss. In the past you have not done this, but instead have played right through your stop loss. Visualize yourself walking away from the tables and going out onto the boardwalk or out into the sunshine and taking a walk.

You can also do the opposite and visualize yourself stopping after your win goal has been accomplished. Suppose your goal is to win $500 for the weekend. See yourself winning the $500, terminating your gambling activities and enjoying the pool and sunshine for the rest of the weekend. Or visualize the win, getting into your car and driving home. Each visualization should take no more than 1 or 2 minutes.

Step 4: Execute Your Game Plan

I would like you to get the idea of a Trip Plan - a plan that schedules your entire trip be it a weekend, a day or a week. Lay it out on paper and schedule your gambling sessions on a daily basis. Start each day with the time you arise and end with the time you go to bed. List the casinos you intend to play and the duration of each playing session.

Document this plan and follow it. It will put you in control of your gambling activities. When you do this once and execute the plan successfully, you will understand the benefits, especially in getting control of your emotions. What you want to accomplish with this step is to play according to your schedule and your requirements and not the casinos.

Step 5: Monitor and Evaluate Your Game Plan

This is a very important step because, without updating and feedback, what is the value of your plan? What this involves is keeping a table by table record of your casino play. For example, let's say you play a craps table. What was your bankroll going into the table? How long did you play? How much did you win or lose? What was your betting unit? Carry a pocket notebook and document these items <u>immediately</u> <u>after playing each table</u>! If your goal is to become a winner, you must do this and you must make it a habit. It only takes a few seconds after each table but the pay offs are great. Now you can evaluate your play in an unemotional, detached manner after each session. You can determine how well you followed your plan and what problems you encountered. The satisfaction you will derive from following this simple procedure will amaze you. Try it!

Here is a review of the column headings for your notebook:

Date and Time; Casino; Game Played (i.e. blackjack, craps, etc.); Starting Session Bankroll; Money Won or Lost; Time Played; Ending Session Bankroll; Cumulative Money Won or Lost; Cumulative Time Played; Comments On Play

First Hour Of Play And Last Hour Of Play

In keeping with the philosophy of controlling your emotions during your gambling sessions, I am going to give you some very valuable advice: don't play during the first hour of your trip and don't play during the last hour of your trip. It has been my experience that this is when the gamblers' intentions are weakest.

Think back ... how many times have you rushed in during that first hour, adrenalin pumping, and played at the first table you've come to? And started out your session with a heavy loss? How many times have you tried to recoup during a last hour and ended up losing more? Or ended up giving back a good portion of your win because you were greedy and going for the kill? No more! Don't play during these critical times! If you don't believe me, at least give it a try. Talk to some of your gambling friends and take a little poll.

What do you do during these time periods? For the first hour stroll around the casino. Look at the gamblers. Look at the tables. Notice how many people are losing. Notice how many people, unlike yourself, have lost control of their emotions and are chasing losses. I recommend not drinking during this first hour. A little alcohol is the easiest way to lose control. But I'm here for fun, you say. Winning, my friend, is more fun than drinking. Besides you can have one or two drinks after your session. If you drink during your session and insist on an alcoholic beverage, I recommend beer, wine or a mixed drink in a tall glass.

During your last hour sit back and enjoy your win. Don't be tempted to give any back. Have a drink or two and relax. Look forward to your next trip. Review your mistakes and the things you did right. Go over your documentation and record your thoughts and impressions in your gambling diary. If you're down for the trip, it's even more important that you don't play during this last hour. Tell yourself that there will always be another day, that the casinos will be there waiting for you when you return. Enjoy the fact that you have your emotions totally in check.

Two very, very important hours. Try my recommendations. They work, I promise you.

Write down your initial thoughts about your goals below.

CHAP 12: THE CASINO GAMBLERS' NETWORK^{tm}

For only $31 you receive at least $100 back in casino coupons plus products and services that are vital to maintaining your winning edge!

Luxury and power permeate the casino environment. Excitement flows with each toss of the dice, spin of the wheel, pull of the handle and deal of the cards. The atmosphere is charged with expectation. Every gambler expects to win and be the "lucky one" to take home a piece of the casino's bankroll.

But take a look around at the extravagant decor, the colors and sounds are all intended to create this exciting environment that gets the adrenalin pumping. The casinos are armed with a host of techniques to separate you from your money as painlessly as possible. Like using chips for example. Think about it. Gamblers have less of a problem losing chips than they would real money. "After all, they're only chips."

But when the day or weekend is over and you are on the way home without your money and possibly facing a big credit card bill at the end of the month, reality sets in!

You need some weapons of your own to chip away at the casino's bankroll and take a slice out for yourself once in a while. The answer is called *The Casino Gamblers' Network*^{tm}.

Have you ever experienced the joy of winning? The shear adrenalin high that comes with grabbing two or three times your pocket bankroll and going home with this money? Of beating the casinos three or four or more trips in succession?

This is what *The Casino Gamblers' Network*^{tm} is all about. Let me tell you more about it.

What The Network Will Do For You

The Casino Gamblers' Network^{tm} offers extraordinary benefits to occasional and frequent gamblers for the modest annual fee of just $39 ($31 for the first year as part of this Charter Membership offer):

- <u>Casino Coupons for at least $100</u> of discounts

- <u>Certified Systems & Methods</u> to enhance your winning edge

- <u>Gamblers' Clinics</u> to instruct, inform, entertain and exchange information that is vital to achieving more winning sessions and holding losing sessions to a minimum

- <u>Gamblers' Connection</u> to bring together gamblers with like interests

- <u>Gamblers' Hotline</u> To inform you where the best games are and where the best video poker payoffs are

- <u>Gamblers' Newsletter</u> to publish certified systems and other important, gambling related information

- <u>Learning Packages</u> to make learning and using basic strategy and counting easy

- <u>Gambling Tours And Adventures</u> to out-of-the-way locations such as Reno/Tahoe; Calgary and Deadwood City

I have many reasons for establishing the Network. Before I relate them to you, let me give you more details on the benefits of this unique idea.

Benefits Of The Casino Gambler's Network[tm]

All of the benefits you derive from the Network, explained below, are available to you after you pay a modest Charter Membership Fee of just $31. Following your first year of membership, your annual membership fee is just $39 (if you decide to renew).

Each of these components is briefly discussed below. If you wish to join the Network, just return the enclosed coupon with your Charter Membership Fee of $31 plus $3 for postage and handling and we will immediately send you your package of materials including all benefits described below. Or, if you prefer and have a major credit card, give us a call, TOLL FREE, at 1-800-257-7130. In New Jersey call 1-609-772-2721.

Casino Coupons Worth At Least $100 in Discounts

We have invited casinos in Atlantic City, Las Vegas and Reno with good playing conditions to present you with a package of discount coupons. The total value of these packages varies depending on location and which casinos are offering the best playing conditions at the time you join but will be at least $100.

Certified Systems & Methods

Money management ideas, systems and methods are submitted to us continuously for evaluation. We will send you three methods, carefully selected and certified, as a bonus for joining *The Casino Gamblers' Network*[tm].

One is a blackjack method with a simple count of the low cards. Using this method you will know whether or not you have advantage on the next hand to be played.

A craps method is included with this package that is called "Going With The Flow." It is designed to keep you in tune with the table cycle with good winning potential on either a hot or a cold table.

A roulette system zeros in those sectors of the wheel that may be recurring more often on a short-term basis.

Used properly, these systems and methods complement those in this book and are certified to improve your chances of winning while holding your losses to a minimum.

Gamblers' Clinics

These Clinics are offered periodically and at no cost in both Nevada and Atlantic City. The clinics will be keyed to both beginning and experienced gamblers. They feature tips and ideas on how to develop and maintain the casino gambler's winning edge. Various systems and methods will be discussed and all of your questions will be answered. The purposes of the clinics are not only to disseminate practical and usable information but also to provide gamblers with a means of connecting with other gamblers with a common interest. For example if you are a blackjack player, you may like to meet other blackjack players who are using the same methods.

In addition to hearing me speak, you will hear other professional gamblers, system developers and members with ideas to share.

Gamblers' Hotline

The purpose of the hotline is to inform you of which casinos offer the best playing conditions. In **Blackjack**, playing conditions are determined by rules of play and other factors discussed in this book. For example when the Claridge in Atlantic City offered the surrender decision, this was reported on our hotline along with the correct strategy for when and when not to surrender.

In **Craps**, your pass line advantage is determined by the free odds bet - single odds, double odds, triple odds or more - the higher the odds, the lower the casinos' advantage. The Hotline keeps you posted.

And in **Roulette**, single-zero wheels are one factor in minimizing the house advantage and the Surrender decision is the other. The Hotline keeps you posted on where to find these favorable conditions.

The odds of winning on **Video Poker** machines vary greatly among the casinos. We will inform you of those casinos which offer the best pay offs and of those casinos whose <u>Video Poker Jackpots are greater than the 4000 coin normal pay off for the royal flush</u>.

And, if we get reports of a biased **Keno** game, you will know about it as soon as we do.

Gamblers' Newsletter

It has been our experience over a 30 year playing career and a 12 + year teaching career that the best source of new ideas for enhancing your winning advantage comes from other gamblers. You would be amazed at how many gamblers have developed their own unique winning systems and methods.

Many gamblers use their specialized skills in computers and statistics to develop systems. Others use common sense approaches that, in many cases, are just as good as a statistical-based method.

Now some systems submitted are worthless but many actually work and are quite useful in the real world of casino play. We encourage our members to submit their ideas, systems and methods for evaluation by our **System Certification Board** and if appropriate, we will disseminate them to you in The Gamblers' Newsletter.

In addition to the publication of certified systems and methods and the evaluation of other published systems, the Newsletter will publish reviews of gambling books and provide you with newly developed tips and ideas from me and other members.

The Newsletter will inform you of all of my instructional activities. We offer a number of proprietary winning methods that are offered in easy-to-learn and use Home Study Courses and, in some cases, in the classroom. Full details are included in Chapter 13 herein.

Learning Packages

You receive a Basic Strategy Learning Package containing a report, flash cards and drills to facilitate the learning process and a wallet-sized card that you can use right inside the casino. Your Card Counting

Learning Package contains easy-to-use drills and exercises for learning the High-Low Point Count System.

Gambling Tours And Adventures.

In our opinion Reno/Tahoe, Nevada is the most interesting and exciting gambling area in the world. And we speak from experience because we've been to most gambling areas. Combine the beauty of the lake and mountains with excellent gambling conditions and the fascinating history of The Comstock Lode gold and silver mining historic area and you have all the makings of a gambling adventure. We will host this guided tour and offer you the opportunity of joining us. Depending upon member interest future tours will include The Calgary Stampede and Deadwood City, South Dakota (legalized gambling in an "old west" town.) As you can see we like to go to "out-of-the-way" places and, if you are interested, we would like to take you with us. . Note: unlike the other benefits, there will be an extra fee for this service.

Charter Membership Offer

The Casino Gamblers' Network^{tm} is an idea whose time has come. The benefits you derive will far outweigh your modest Charter Membership Fee of $31 (which covers your membership for the first 12 months; the annual renewel fee is just $39 if you decide to renew).

The Casino Coupons themselves give you a value of at least $100.

The Certified Systems & Methods have a market value of at least $50 to $100 each. You get them at no cost and and they will definitely increase your chances of winning and hold your losing sessions to a minimum.

If you don't get at least one tip from your first Gamblers' Clinic that is worth at least $31 in your opinion, I will be happy to refund your Charter Membership Fee on the spot.

What is the value of the Gamblers' Hotline which provides you up-to-date information on where to find the best games and how to avoid the worst games? Our users tell us it saves them both time and dollars and makes them money when they find a good game to exploit.

And, The Gambler's Newsletter, providing you an ongoing source of winning tips, ideas, certified systems and methods, delivers value many times the amount of your small membership fee. Similar newsletters covering blackjack alone are sold for $95 and higher a year.

In fact any of these products and services are worth more than your annual membership fee. So even if you can't make the clinics or are not interested in a new system or method, you should consider joining for those benefits that will enhance your winning edge.

So please send in your Registration Form today. Every day you wait could be costing you money in the form of avoidable losses in the casino.

You will receive a written confirmation including a statement of Network policies and operational procedures for submitting your ideas, systems and methods for evaluation (if you choose to do so; submitting a system is not a requirement for membership).

Jerry is also accepting applications for membership on **The System Certification Board.** A form is included with your membership materials.

You will also receive:

- Casino Discount Coupons worth at least $100

- Three Certified Systems & Methods documented in a special edition of The Gambler's Newsletter. The Gambler's Newsletter is not on a specific publication schedule but you will receive at least two more copies, and probably three, during your membership year.

- A Basic Strategy Learning Package including wallet-sized card and training materials

- A Card-Counting Learning Package including drills and exercises for learning the High-Low Count

- A Schedule Of Gambler's Clinics

- A telephone number and access code for the Gamblers' Hotline

- An invitation to the next gambling tour and adventure

Your satisfaction with *The Casino Gamblers' Network*^{tm} and your membership materials is completely guaranteed. If you are dissatisfied for any reason, your money will be refunded.

Why The Casino Gamblers' Network^{tm} Was Established

I have been active for over 25 years in developing and validating systems and methods to beat the casinos. My research started in 1961 with the first ever computer model to simulate the game of blackjack.

In addtion to my research and development activities, our students and clients have been submitting systems and methods to us for evaluation for a number of years. We get one or two new ideas every week and at least one new documented system submitted every month. We evaluate them and we ask our clients and graduates to help us evaluate them. The good ones are circulated and the bad ones are junked.

All systems and methods submitted are evaluated by a **System Certification Board**. This Board, appointed by Jerry, includes specialists in computer software and statistical analysis. It also includes gamblers like yourself who are willing to work the method at home and try it out, under fire, in the casino.

The System Certification Board will either certify the system or not, depending on it's evaluation of the system's effectiveness and other important criteria.

So you are not getting a rehash of systems in other books or systems pedaled by system sellers! You are the recipient of certified systems and methods that yield the highest chances of winning, that help you to attain the casino gambler's winning edge.

The Casino Gamblers' Network has existed, informally, for a number of years. The idea of expanding the Network and making it available to other gamblers has been considered for quite some time but it had to be done in the right way. To keep the membership fee low and also to make it easy to operate, we did not want to "advertise it to the world." We wanted to open it up to gamblers who are familiar with us and would seek us out. Thus originated the idea of using this book as the announcement media.

There are other reasons why *The Casino Gambler's Network*[tm] was formed. One, quite frankly, is ego. I enjoy speaking to gamblers and sharing my expertise. We used to do two-hour blackjack clinics in cities around the country and the give- and-take, the questions and answers, the dissemination of useful information were very satisfying activities for both of us.

But these got to be too much work and kept me away from the tables. I had to answer the question: "Am I a teacher or a professional gambler?" The gambler in me won.

I look forward to presenting The Gamblers' Clinics that are part of your Network because they are scheduled only 3-4 times per year for Atlantic City, Las Vegas and Reno/Tahoe. So we can deliver them cost-effectively (we are all there to gamble anyway, aren't we?).

The botton line is information. We are in business to deliver information to gamblers that will save them money, make them money and enhance their fun and enjoyment in the casino.

Information equals power. The power of ideas and systems and methods that yield profits. *The Casinos Gamblers' Network*^{tm} is your winning edge over the casinos!

CHAPTER 13: PRODUCTS AND SERVICES OFFERED BY JERRY PATTERSON

This section describes books, home study courses and classes that I have developed for those interested in acquiring additional knowledge for beating the casinos.

Although an active professional gambler spending much of my time at the blackjack tables and managing my investments in the stock and commodity futures options markets, I am committed to serving the needs of beginning, intermediate and experienced gamblers. This is accomplished through *The Casino Gamblers' Network*[tm] described in Chapter 12 and by offering the products and services described in this Chapter.

1. Blackjack Books by Jerry Patterson

Use the coupon on the last page to order these books if you can't find them at your local bookstore.

Blackjack: A Winner's Handbook

This book contains a review of the entire blackjack field including blackjack books, card-counting systems, newsletters and magazines, and instructional programs. Written in 1977 and revised and expanded in 1982, this book is still a must for the serious player's library. A plan for player development is included which offers beginning, intermediate, and advanced programs. The book includes a complete and comprehensive bibliography.

Break the Dealer

Published in 1986, *Break The Dealer* provides information never before published on the different shuffles and how they affect your game. The book describes a number of subtle changes in the game of blackjack that have hurt traditional blackjack players and card-counters.

Break The Dealer offers easy-to-understand chapters on basic blackjack strategy and card counting. The book describes how to detect the type of shuffle a casino is using, and explains what it means to your game. You'll find specific advice on how to find a favorable shuffle and learn the best - and worst - times to play blackjack in a casino - and why.

For the serious blackjack player there is a chapter on shuffle-tracking. This technique, never published before, describes the card-counting method of tracking a clump of tens through the shuffle and cutting it into play in the next shoe.

Blackjack's Winning Formula

This book is a primer for the student who desires to beat the game. It explains the rudiments of the game for the novice player. The book includes basic strategy, card-counting, and money management techniques for both Atlantic City and Nevada. Some of my and my team's blackjack adventures in Nevada, Atlantic City and the Caribbean are highlighted. Excellent chapters are included that point up the advantages of the female blackjack player.

2. The TARGET Instructional Program

The TARGET Method was described in Chapter 6. It is offered both as a Home Study Course or a Weekend Class Experience in Atlantic City, Las Vegas or Reno/Tahoe.

The TARGET Home Study Course includes **audio and video tape instruction, training manuals and telephone consultation**. It features in-casino instruction with a small group of students conducted by me or one of my instructors. In addition, TARGET Update Seminars are offered periodically. TARGET is a unique instructional program and your inquiries are invited. Please call my office **TOLL FREE** for a **FREE 12-page brochure** or use the coupon at the back of this chapter to request one.

TARGET Course Outline

<u>Lesson 1: Understanding TARGET And Why You Win</u>

- How to Select a Money-Making Table

- How One TARGET Superfactor Can Almost Guarantee Your Profits

- When to Leave the Table with Profits in Hand

- How and Why TARGET Solves the Problems Associated with Card-Counting

- How to Use TARGET to Pick Tables Where the Count Really Works

- Definitions of Bias and Nonrandom Shuffles and How They Work to Your Advantage

- Why the "Wash" Makes Certain Games Off-Limits

- Understanding the Different Types of Shuffles and How They Work to Your Advantage or Disadvantage

- Special Drills for TARGET Casino Practice.

Lesson 2: Exploiting TARGET's Profit Potential

- Questions and Answers From a Live TARGET Classroom Session

- How to Increase Your Profits by Using a Disciplined Documentation Method

- Money Management: Flat Betting (Betting the Same Amount) and When to Use It

- Money Management: When to Bet and When Not to Bet with the Count

- Money Management: Special Techniques for Recreational Gamblers, High Rollers and Junket Players

- Tips for Creating the "Home Run Tables" Where the Dealer Breaks Hand After Hand

- How to "Tune" Your Play to Exploit the Special Advantages in the Atlantic City Game

- Nuances for the Variety of Games in Nevada

- "Action TARGET": Amazing Money-Making Opportunities for Nevada's Single-Deck Games

- When and How to Avoid Losing by Standing on Stiff Hands

- How to Evaluate a Casino for TARGET Play

Lesson 3: Casino Session (Two hours in the casino with Jerry and a small group)

- How the Casino Session Works

- Instructor Selects TARGET Tables for Review and Comment

- Students Practice Scouting and Table Selection with Instructor Feedback

- Instructor Monitors Table Departure

151

TARGET course materials include (1) six hours of audiocassette tapes; (2) two hours of video tape; (3) target training manual; (4) a portfolio of expanded target course materials; (5) Basic Strategy course materials; (6) Card-Counting course materials; (7) Casino Evaluation Report; (8) access to TARGET Hotline; (9) follow-up: consultation, conferences and TARGET Update Seminars.

Also included with the TARGET Course is a complete course on mental discipline, including manual, audio tapes and a 21- day preparatory program, including self inventory and daily success diary

Call for a FREE brochure or to order the TARGET Course. Or send us the Information Request Coupon at the back of this chapter.

Please note that if you decide to order this unique instructional program, you take absolutely no risk because you are protected by an unconditional and legally binding guarantee.

3. Computer-assisted Blackjack Tutor

Custom-designed for use with most personal computers, the Computer-Assisted Blackjack Tutor will enable a player with just elementary knowledge of basic strategy, card counting and money management to become a highly skilled card counter. The program includes the High-Low Card Counting System - easiest to learn, easiest to play, used by more advanced counting method for efficiency. The player may set parameters to describe the type of blackjack game he wishes to play: number of decks, number of players, cut-card placement, money management strategy and many others. You are invited to request a free brochure. Use the Information Request Coupon.

4. Other Products And Services

I am a Registered Investment Advisor specializing in ferreting out and exploiting opportunities in the speculative financial markets: options on stocks, options on futures and low priced stocks.

Your inquiries are invited.

REGISTRATION FORM:

THE CASINO GAMBLERS' NETWORK^{TM}

Please remove this page from book and send it or a copy to:

Jerry Patterson

1133 Thackary Ct., Box 777

Voorhees, NJ 08043

FOR FASTER SERVICE CALL TOLL FREE:
1-800-257-7130.
IN NEW JERSEY CALL: 1-609-772-2721.

Dear Jerry,

Enclosed is my $31 Registration Fee plus $3 for postage and handling for a total of $34. Please enroll me immediately in *The Casino Gamblers' Network*^{tm}.

I understand that my membership entitles me to all the benefits, products and services described in Chapter 12 of this book and that they will be shipped upon your receipt of this membership form.

I further understand that if I am dissatisfied in any way, that you will refund my $31 Charter Membership fee at any time during my one-year membership. I understand that the renewel fee for my second year, should I desire to renew, is just $39.

Please print name and address on back of this page.

Name:_____

Street Address:_____

City/State/Zip:_____

Credit Card Number: _____

Daytime Phone: _____

Check Enclosed For: $_____

INFORMATION REQUEST FORM

Please remove this page from book and send it or a copy to:

Jerry Patterson
1133 Thackary Ct; Box 777
Voorhees, NJ 08043

FOR FASTER SERVICE CALL TOLL FREE:
1-800-257-7130
IN NEW JERSEY CALL: 1-609- 772-2721.

Please send me a FREE brochure on the following:

[   ] Home Study Course with audio and video tapes on the Blackjack TARGET Method

[   ] A Schedule Of Weekend Blackjack Classes taught by Jerry Patterson

[   ] Computer-Assisted Blackjack Tutor

[   ] Information on your Financial Advisory Service for options on stocks, options on futures and low priced stocks

[   ] Please call me at the telephone number below and tell me about a simple demonstration of a blackjack table bias that will show me how your TARGET program works.

For a FREE brochure please call today.

Name:_____

Street Address: _____

City/State/Zip: _____

Telephone Number: _____

ORDER FORM FOR JERRY PATTERSON'S BLACKJACK BOOKS

Please remove this page from book and send it or a copy to:

> Jerry Patterson
> 1133 Thackary Ct., Box 777
> Voorhees, NJ 08043

FOR FASTER SERVICE CALL TOLL FREE:
1-800-257-7130
IN NEW JERSEY CALL 1-609- 772-2721.

Please send me the books I have checked below. I understand the price of each is $8 plus $3 for first-class shipping and handling for a total of $11 per book.

[ ] Blackjack: A Winner's Handbook.

[ ] Break The Dealer

[ ] Blackjack's Winning Formula

Please fill out name, address and other data on back of this page.

Total Amount Enclosed: $_____

Credit Card Number: _____•_____

Exp. Date:_____

Daytime Phone (for credit card orders): _____

Name:_____

Street Address:_____

City/State/Zip:_____